Gunship
Over Angola

Gunship
Over Angola
The Story of a Maverick Pilot

Steve Joubert

Delta Books
Johannesburg & Cape Town

Originally published in South Africa in 2019 by
DELTA BOOKS
A division of Jonathan Ball Publishers
A division of Media24 (Pty) Ltd
PO Box 33977
Jeppestown
2043

ISBN 978-1-86842-930-1
ebook ISBN 978-1-86842-931-8

*Every effort has been made to trace the copyright holders and to obtain their
permission for the use of copyright material. The publishers apologise for any
errors or omissions and would be grateful to be notified of any corrections that
should be incorporated in future editions of this book.*

Twitter: https://twitter.com/DeltaBooksSA
Facebook: https://www.facebook.com/DeltaBooksSA/
Blog: http://jonathanball.bookslive.co.za/

Design and typesetting by Baseline Publishing Services
Editing by Alfred LeMaitre
Proofreading by Joan Cameron
Set in ITC Berkeley Oldstyle Std 11.5 on 15pt

To Diane,

my anchor, my greatest critic and my best friend

I now know why men who have been to war yearn to reunite. Not to tell stories or look at old pictures. Not to laugh or weep. Comrades gather because they long to be with the men who once acted their best, men who suffered and sacrificed, who were stripped raw ... right down to their humanity.

– Ray Haakonsen

Contents

Author's note

It is often said that 'writing about it' is one of the most cathartic things that human beings who have undergone extreme trauma can do. I firmly believe this, and can personally testify to the truthfulness of that statement. Often, while writing this book, I sat down at my laptop to continue writing but nothing of any substance was forthcoming. I'd try in vain for ten minutes, 20 and sometimes even longer until suddenly, like a veil being drawn back to reveal the scene, I was back in the cockpit and the sights, sounds and smells were as they'd been more than 35 years ago.

As I've aged, I have felt compelled to tell some of the story of my life and, by doing so, to end my family's practice of stoically avoiding telling its own history and forcing those who might be interested in the subject, like me, to delve into obscure inscriptions in centuries-old family bibles and piles of sepia-tinted photographs to decipher our origins.

I have five children, a son-in-law, a daughter-in-law and three granddaughters who, I must admit, haven't yet become avid fans of my writing, but who I hope, in years to come, might spend some time reading my story.

'How long have you wanted to be a pilot?'

The plastic chair stood in the centre of a sprung wooden floor in a large room in a nondescript building at the South African Air Force Gymnasium in Valhalla, Pretoria. Spread around it in a semicircle were 13 office chairs, in which sat an intimidating collection of 12 senior officers of the South African Air Force (SAAF) and a single brigadier representing the South African Medical Services (SAMS). In front of each officer was a desk.

Outside this room, waiting for the command to enter, was me, 74257684BC Private Stephen Pierre Joubert, national serviceman (NSM) and aspirant military aviator.

The door opened and a voice, with a clear tinge of sadism, said, 'It's your turn. Go!'

My heart, which was already thumping like a V-twin Harley-Davidson at full throttle, immediately tried to burst free from my pounding chest. I stepped gingerly onto the threshold, aiming, as I'd practised over and over again in the days leading up to this moment, first to pause for a second or two, calmly gather my thoughts, and allow my eyes to adjust to the comparative gloom before I entered to face the inquisition within.

But, in my blind panic, all I saw was the empty chair, and like a condemned convict fixated on the noose that will shortly change the direction of his life, I headed straight for it without hesitating. Six inches from the chair I realised with morbid certainty that I had miscalculated the distance and impact was unavoidable and inevitable. When my right knee, while crashing to a military-grade halt, thumped into the back of the chair, the concomitant

3

transfer of kinetic energy caused the fragile piece of furniture to launch dangerously towards the general sitting directly in front of me.

In a moment of surprising eye-hand coordination, my right hand shot out in a partially successful attempt to prevent the chair hitting one of the innocent observers, but in doing so I upended the wretched thing. It crashed thunderously onto the wooden floor.

The noise echoed around the sparsely furnished room.

Flustered, I bent over to set the errant object right side up, but in so doing my cap fell to the floor. I frantically jammed it back on my head while still bent over and only then stood up.

In a moment that I will remember forever, I came face to face with General Bob Rogers, decorated veteran of the Second World War and the Korean War, legendary aviator, then Chief of the SAAF and the chairman of the SAAF Pilot Selection Board.

I lifted my right hand to salute him, just like I'd been trained to do.

But instead of the peak of my cap being at eye level, it was pointing steeply skywards at a 45-degree angle, like that of a bus driver. The intended salute (touch the tip of your right index finger to the peak, my boy) couldn't be completed correctly under the present conditions. I compromised, but in doing so only served to make the picture even more ludicrous. My hand hovered in the space between where it should have been and where the peak was, making my attempt at paying respects look like a watered-down Heil Hitler.

I stood there mortified, my mouth slightly agape and changing colour like a chameleon on a box of Smarties.

Inside my chest, feelings of despair were already oozing out. It was the most important day of my young life and I'd blown it ... and I hadn't even opened my mouth yet.

Blinking furiously, I tried to gauge the situation, my desperate gaze seeking a hint of encouragement from any one of the assembled brass, but in vain. In addition to General Rogers, there was at least one more general, perhaps two, a bevy of brigadiers and a collection of colonels.

Their faces stared back, deadpan. No one cracked even the slightest smile, despite the unintentional vaudeville farce being enacted right in front of them. Instead they all looked at me as I imagined they would a blob of sticky dog turd accidentally attached to the toe of their perfectly polished shoes.

After what seemed like an age, General Rogers finally spoke.

'Have you finished?' he asked brightly.

He was answered by a voice that sounded vaguely like mine, had I just been punched hard in the larynx.

'I think so, sir.'

'Then try to pretend for a moment that you're not driving a tram, take off your cap and sit down,' he said.

I sat forlornly in that seat, certain that I'd just tossed out the window the career that I'd dreamt about since I was a small boy.

In anticipation of facing the selection board that day, I'd had my formal uniform dry-cleaned, pressed to a parade-ground crispness, I had polished my shoes to a mirror-like sheen, and shone my brass buttons and cap-mounted eagle so bright that one risked eye damage looking directly at them.

The preceding weeks had been a whirl of medical examinations, with assorted specialists probing and prodding every nook and cranny and psychologists trying to establish if I was psychologically equipped to be a flyboy. I'd seen 90 per cent of the guys who'd started the final selection process with me get eliminated for even the slightest aberration. Some, on hearing the news of their rejection, had stood rooted to the spot, sobbing with frustration and disappointment before being led away by friends and colleagues.

We were told, and I didn't know if this was fact, that 7 500 young men had applied to become SAAF pilots in the current intake (at the time the SAAF selected pilot trainees twice a year). Only 700 of them had been invited to the medical evaluation process, and there were just 115 of us facing the final stage, the Pilot Selection Board.

All I'd done and all I'd experienced had led up to this moment, and in a matter of a seconds I had misjudged the distance to the chair and set this career-terminating disaster in motion.

In that situation, I reverted to the only defence I knew – I'd make them laugh.

So, when the General asked the first question, 'How long have you wanted to be a pilot?', instead of giving the expected answer, 'Ever since I can remember, General', I said, 'Since I stopped wanting to be an ice-cream seller, sir!'

'An ice-cream seller? Please explain,' the General said, somewhat taken aback.

'Well, sir, when I was very little, I thought the greatest job in the world was that of the guy driving the bicycle with the bin of Dairy Maid ice creams through the neighbourhood. Since that dream faded, I wanted to be a pilot.'

'Not much ambition there,' he muttered, more to himself than to anyone else.

'On the contrary, sir,' I said, and his eyebrows arched.

'Explain?'

In for a penny, in for a pound, I thought.

'Don't get too comfortable in that chair, sir. I'd like to sit there some day!'

A funereal silence followed.

'Does anyone have any questions to ask this young man?' the General asked the other officers in the room, confirming, as if I hadn't already known, that he was done with me.

From the left, someone asked, 'How does a jet engine work?'

'The air comes in the front, gets compressed and heated and shot out the back,' I offered hopefully, while suspecting that this particular level of brevity was unlikely to win anyone over.

'Anyone else? No? Thank you. You can go.' This statement was made without even a hint of hesitation between the words.

I got groggily to my feet, replaced my cap, fashioned a salute, this time more like how I'd been taught to do it, then spun around so quickly that the sole of my shoe under the ball of my left foot struck a raised joint between two planks and stopped turning! There was an audible crack from the area of my ankle.

'I say, are you all right?' inquired General Rogers.

'Fine ... urgghh, thanks ... sir!' I gasped through tightly clenched jaws as I came close to passing out from the excruciating pain in my left leg.

Somehow, I managed to stagger from the room, blinded by embarrassment, despair, frustration and dismay. So ended possibly the shortest Pilot Selection Board interview in the history of the SAAF.

Part I
The age of innocence

1

A rebel is born

Those who have come to know me through my life are patently aware that I am not a military man at heart. I also come from a long line of non-military-minded men, the first of whom to arrive in South Africa was a rebellious-minded but principled French Huguenot called Pierre Jaubert (the a soon became an o). He hailed from La Motte-d'Aigues in Provence in the south of France and arrived at the Cape in 1688 aboard the Dutch East India Company ship *Berg China.*

The ancestors that I have been able to trace were all conscripts or volunteers in times of war. My great-grandfather fought on the side of the Boers in the Anglo-Boer War, and both my grandfathers served in the Second World War. Uncle Joffre, my grandfather's brother, was a navigator on Liberators and Mosquitos during the Second World War and played a role in the Allied supply drops during the Warsaw Uprising of 1944. I met him a few times as a young boy and was struck by his boundless energy, which bordered on, and sometimes exceeded, the bounds of sanity. I recall that he was married seven times and that he also crashed motor cars with some regularity. And Dad did a few months of national service in Northern Rhodesia (now Zambia) with the British Army.

Apart from these family members, why do I not consider myself to be a military man? Well, for one thing, I question everything, a trait that will not make you too many friends in high places in the military hierarchy anywhere in the world. I also struggle with carrying out orders that don't have a rational expectation attached.

*

I was born in Chingola on the Copperbelt in Northern Rhodesia on 3 July 1958. My dad was born in Pretoria and named Pierre after the original Huguenot ancestor. My mom was Inez (née Wilson) and she was born in Brakpan but would never admit to that fact, preferring instead to say that she was born 'near to Johannesburg'. Dad's family had moved to the Copperbelt immediately after the Second World War and both Grandpa and Gran worked at Nchanga copper mine in Chingola.

My mom, who was in all likelihood a direct descendant of King George IV, albeit from illegitimate lineage, was halfway through her matric year at Guinea Fowl School in Gwelo in Southern Rhodesia on the day she turned 16 in July 1950. Her parents, who'd divorced when she was only four, seem to have cared little for her, and she was shuttled off to various boarding schools after the divorce. On that day, a telegram arrived at the school, instructing her to use the small amount in the accompanying postal order to purchase a train ticket and return home to Brakpan, where her mother, who was living there with a new husband, would help her to find gainful employment.

Mom was in her final year of schooling and just months away from completing her matric, a rarity for a young woman in those days, but this seems not to have mattered to her mother. Bitterly angered and disappointed by this dismissal of her academic aspirations, and with no viable alternative, Mom caught the train from Gwelo to Bulawayo the next day.

Bulawayo was the junction where the railway line going south to Johannesburg met the one going west towards Francistown, in Bechuanaland (now Botswana). In Bulawayo, it was necessary for Mom to change from the westbound train to a southbound service for the final leg of the journey home. True to her independent nature, and to protest the anger that she felt for her parents, when she reached Bulawayo she walked boldly up to the ticket office and asked, 'How far north does the train from Johannesburg travel?'

The three-toothed man in the ticket office replied: 'To the edge of beyond, my sweetie!'

'That's good enough for me!' she said, and promptly bought a ticket to Chingola, where the northbound line terminated.

Emerging from Chingola station late the following afternoon, she found a nearby boarding house run by a young couple, Ben and Hazel Rens. They immediately adopted her.

Mom quickly adapted to the frontier nature of the town and got a job in the assay lab at the Nchanga copper mine. Her boss, Una Joubert, had a son, Pierre, who was just finishing his own matric at Grey College in Bloemfontein. Not long afterwards, introductions were made, she and my dad became an item, and they married on 12 December 1954.

Debbie was born first, 'prematurely', six months later. Then there was a reasonable two-year gap before Jacqueline was born. I followed 13 months later, and Mark followed barely ten months after that. My mom had her last three kids in 23 months!

Legend has it that my dad, upon learning of my birth – my being the first boy after two daughters (somehow that was important then) – instead of going to the hospital as a new father would today, set off with his best friend, John 'Buck' Jones, into the bush, with the intention of hunting and dispatching a trophy buffalo/sable/roan/elephant to mark the momentous occasion of my emergence into the world.

This was not an unusual practice, as the matron of the Chingola hospital, like many people at the time, felt that fathers were an unnecessary impediment to the birthing and neonatal phases. Men were not permitted in the maternity ward, let alone the delivery room, and so disappearing into the bush for a few days with one's mates at the birth of one's progeny was nothing unusual.

Dad and Buck were accompanied on the hunting expedition by Peter Chibemba, the manager of our household. Before they left, the trio cleared out the local bottle store of all available stocks of brandy and beer, which they imbibed with abandon on the way to and from the hunting grounds. In their thoroughly inebriated state, they proceeded to wage war on the wildlife that inhabited the untamed border area in their quest to harvest the trophy of trophies – with no clear idea what they were looking for! Many, many rounds (of ammunition, brandy and beer) later, and with nothing to show for it but four-day stubble and extreme body odour, they came to the considered opinion that they should return to relative civilisation and make my acquaintance in person.

Being in a fairly intoxicated state, and with a desire to enjoy the return journey sitting or lying on the Land Rover's bonnet and on its roof, they told Peter Chibemba to drive the vehicle. Peter was only marginally acquainted with engines and gears on a wheeled vehicle. Nevertheless, being the least sozzled of the trio, and despite causing all kinds of damage to the vehicle, road signs and assorted passing village architecture, he somehow managed to guide the vehicle back to Chingola, but not without running over and killing a stray goat while negotiating a dirt track through some obscure hamlet.

Triumphantly, the freshly expired goat was lifted up onto the roof of the vehicle by the intrepid trio, and they arrived at the Chingola hospital late at night, tyres squealing and gears grating, in a cloud of suffocating dust, and immediately set about attempting to gain entry thereto. The deceased goat, draped across my dad's shoulders, now represented the originally desired trophy.

Dad's 'gift for my boy' stared vacantly at the unfolding scene.

Understandably denied access by the indignant matron and nursing staff, the trio regrouped and, using their formidable combined intellect, changed strategy. They set off stumbling and guffawing around the hospital perimeter to the maternity section, where they then proceeded to serenade the obstetric wing at the top of their voices while brandishing their 'trophy'.

The song that they sang, somewhat discordantly, but fittingly, was, 'Hang down your head Tom Dooley.' I swear that my first memory is of my mother, laughing uncontrollably, holding me in her arms while standing on the first-floor balcony, looking down fondly at the performance.

*

The surrounding bush played a major role in my toddler years, and I recall with great fondness the lessons in bushcraft taught to me even at that tender age by Dad and Peter. We had at least one bushbaby as a pet, and I also developed a liking for chameleons, each of whom I named Charlie.

Chameleons were not permitted in the house, as they tended to terrify the domestic help. When I smuggled them in, Peter would take them out into the garden and release them at the first available opportunity. I would become distraught when I was unable to find the latest Charlie where I had left him and would begin to cry. Finally, an exasperated Peter would take me into the bush to look for Charlie and, irrespective of whatever chameleon we found, he'd convince me that it was Charlie and peace would return for a time.

I learnt at a young age that a stick of bone-dry hartebeest biltong provided effective relief for teething pains in babies, that anthills invariably contained red ants that bit mercilessly at one's tender parts, and that fathers in that part of Africa never came home early on a Friday evening.

A weekly battle raged in our home at around midnight each Friday when Mom would try to stop Peter from heating my long-overdue Dad's dinner in the oven. Mom would put the plate into the fridge to ensure that the fat would congeal. But, as soon as her back was turned, Peter would take it out of the fridge and return it to the oven. This battle would rage on for hours. Peter was dismissed from our employ at least 15 times every Friday night.

Weekend fishing expeditions to the Kafue River were a regular occurrence and helped give me a deep love for the African bush, which endures to this day. I have one abiding memory from one of these trips.

During this particular adventure, my younger brother Mark, who was but a toddler, had been settled, naked, in the back of our Opel Caravan station wagon to sleep through the heat of the tropical day. Temperatures around the 40°C mark were quite common.

The Opel's tailgate was open, as were all its doors. Somehow a hungry blue vervet monkey got into the back of the car and, while sorting through the buffet of tasty treats on offer, grabbed what he probably thought was a juicy caterpillar, but which turned out to be Mark's willy.

My mom and the other ladies, who were chatting nearby, suddenly saw the monkey in the car, and a great shriek was heard. Mark woke up, saw and no doubt felt the monkey and also started to wail. Alarmed and confused, the monkey joined the cacophony, wondering what was causing the hysteria.

My dad and his mates, hearing the barrage of panic-stricken noise, came running. On seeing the sight before them, they collapsed in a heap on the ground, laughing until they cried, much to the chagrin of Mom and the other ladies.

At that moment, my brother, in an instinctive effort at self-preservation, tried feebly to hit the poor ape, which prompted Buck Jones to comment, 'Isn't Mark a bit young to spank the monkey!'

*

In 1963, when I was five years old, my parents decided to leave Northern Rhodesia and move south. This followed the tragic death of my sister Jacqueline in 1961. She died at our home in Chingola when she fell between two treated poles that formed the apex of a rose arch in our garden. Her little head caught in the gap, preventing her from breathing.

She was just two and a half years old and was buried in the Chingola cemetery. This devastatingly traumatic event, coupled with the rise of Uhuru-related violence against white people in that part of the world, led to our moving to a place where my folks hoped that the agony of Jacqui's passing might be mitigated. Mom and Dad carried the acute pain of her loss for the rest of their lives.

My dad had little intention of going far, but Mom had other ideas. Dad had designs on us settling at Lake Kariba. He was a shoo-in for a job as a ranger in Operation Noah, which was aimed at rescuing animals stranded by the waters rising behind the newly built Kariba Dam. This enormous structure was constructed in a gorge on the Zambezi River, which formed the border between Northern Rhodesia and Southern Rhodesia (today Zimbabwe). Until the day he passed away in 2003, even a mention of Kariba and the Zambezi valley would cause Dad to drift off into a state of melancholy and longing for the African bush and the undying regret that he hadn't played a greater role in its conservation.

As it happened, my mom didn't post his job application to the relevant authorities. Many years later, the discovery, in an old trunk, of this unposted set of documents led to the most epic of rows in the Joubert household, spanning several days at least.

Might this have been an act of revenge on Mom's part, possibly seen in the context of Dad's actions a number of years earlier? Let me explain. When they decided to get married, spurred on by the fact that my eldest sister was definitely going to be born three months 'prematurely', my folks lacked the funds to buy either engagement or wedding rings. It was only after they had been married a few years that they were able to afford a decent wedding band, and so my dad was dispatched to Chingola town to make the long-awaited purchase of the symbol of their marital union.

However, on entering the single-street Chingola central business district and just before reaching the jewellery shop, he passed the Land Rover dealership. A bright, new, short-wheelbase Land Rover was on display.

Had this been a fight, the referee would have ruled 'no contest' within seconds of the opening bell. The price of the Land Rover and the price of the ring were about the only things equal in this one-sided contest. Everything else in the equation was, in Dad's mind, logically weighted. Before long, he was happily driving home in something practical, as opposed to something ornamental ... His arrival at our home at 33 Briar Street in Chingola was not greeted with the same euphoria. It was to carry consequences for which he would pay dearly, right then and in the years to follow.

Self-preservation dictated that he left home a few seconds after arriving, and he did so without clothing, equipment or supplies, his ears ringing from Mom's tirade. He then picked up his friend Buck and went to christen the Rover in the wilderness.

Suffice to say that our destiny as a family was largely determined, some would say, by the unfortunate positioning of two shops on a dusty Copperbelt street!

As our impending departure for South Africa drew closer, Dad got grumpier and grumpier. He ranted and raged about the Rhodesian Wildlife Authority's 'downright rudeness and arrogance', with their failure to confirm his Lake Kariba appointment central to his chagrin. Preparations for the move progressed at an alarming rate with Mom's knowing, but mostly concealed, smile a constant source of friction between them.

Suddenly, the morning of departure dawned and it was time to go. Our Peugeot 404 station wagon, bought new for the occasion by trading in the Opel and the Land Rover, was jam-packed with all manner of household goods and three little wide-eyed kids aged eight (Debbie), five (me) and four (Mark), respectively. The roof rack was piled high with an assortment of chests and trunks covered with a green canvas tarpaulin.

Peter, dressed in his uniform of short white trousers and white shirt, stood barefooted next to the car. In his hand was the tiniest little suitcase you have ever seen.

'Where do I sit?' he asked Dad.

'You can't go with us, Peter,' my father responded.

'Why not?' asked Peter.

'Because the family is moving to South Africa, Peter,' replied my dad firmly.

'But I am family!' he pleaded.

'But this is your home, Peter. South Africa is not,' my mom tried to reason with him.

'My home is with my children and my family,' shouted Peter, 'and you are they!'

For a full ten minutes the exchange raged on, by the second becoming more charged with emotion. Peter couldn't accept that he was not coming with us. The sound of his voice, beseeching first my mom, then my dad, to allow him to sit on the roof for the duration of the 3 000-kilometre journey to South Africa, remains with me to this day.

Finally, with tears flowing freely, and too choked up to say another word, my parents bundled our loudly wailing family into the Peugeot, with Peter standing resolute alongside, tears coursing down his cheeks. We drove off slowly down the road.

I was one of those three little faces staring out of the rear window watching the ever-diminishing image of Peter, tiny suit-case in hand, trotting down the dusty road after us.

He finally disappeared in the cloud of dust kicked up by our car.

*

We entered South Africa on Dingane's Day, 16 December 1963. My paternal grandparents lived on a farm just north of Pretoria, and we joined them there and lived on the farm for a few months.

During this time, I started attending Loreto Convent in Gezina, Pretoria. When Mom picked me up after my first day and asked whether I had enjoyed myself, I let her know quite firmly that 'I didn't mind it but I don't think I need to go back there any more.'

Each day when I got back from school I'd ask Lettie, the housekeeper, whether Peter Chibemba had arrived that morning. When she replied, as she always did, that he hadn't, I would go to the start of the long driveway, which ran down the boundary fence of the farm all the way to the Great North Road a few kilometres away, and stare down it for hours.

I told anyone who asked that I was waiting.

Waiting for Peter to appear.

*

Before too long, my folks bought a house in the suburb of Valhalla, in the southwestern part of Pretoria. Valhalla was where many of the serving military personnel of the South African Defence Force (SADF) lived, due to its close proximity to the vast military complex of Voortrekkerhoogte and the airfields of Air Force Base (AFB) Swartkop and AFB Waterkloof.

Dad went on to forge a successful business career, adjusting surprisingly well to corporate life, but ultimately his desire to be in his own business prevailed and he formed and ran a short-haul construction company right until he died in 2003. My mom was a specialist in state-of-the-art printing techniques and soon joined the Council for Scientific and Industrial Research (CSIR), where she was still employed at the time she passed away so tragically.

From the time we moved to Valhalla in April 1964, Debbie and I would catch the school bus to and from General Andries Brink Primary School in Voortrekkerhoogte, the only primary school in the area that taught in English. I do not remember the exact details of what happened one Friday afternoon in October 1964 while we were on the homeward-bound school bus, but I think it started with our driver failing to heed a stop sign at a T-junction in Valhalla. He turned a corner directly into the path of a large truck carrying a load of enormous cement sewage pipes.

In the carnage that followed the collision between the bus and the truck, thirteen children lost their lives, including the two who were sitting on either side of me. I was pulled from the mangled wreckage by rescuers. I had suffered quite severe head injuries. An ambulance rushed me to Pretoria General Hospital, where I

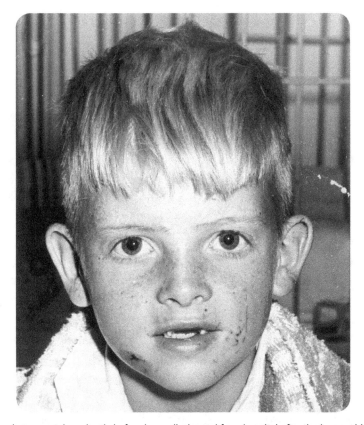

This photo was taken shortly before I was discharged from hospital after the bus accident.

teetered between life and death for a few weeks before ultimately making a full recovery.

The crash left me with a permanent aversion to crowded places. But it also introduced me to my guardian angel, who has hovered around me my whole life.

*

My schooldays went by in a flash of sport, friends and fun. I had a great sense of privilege while growing up, and I don't mean privilege in the material and financial sense of the word. My folks and my friends' parents were neither wealthy nor poor, though they tended towards the latter. 'Dumplings' to fill our bellies and 'bread and scratchit' were regular items on the supper menu, often before the middle of the month.

Our education in the government schooling system was relatively backward by today's standards, and television was not yet a reality. Yet we were wealthy beyond price. For example, just across the road was Laureston Farm, where a dairy herd of approximately 100 cows produced the freshest milk and the richest cream you could imagine. There was also a natural slip-and-slide chute shaped into the black clay on the banks of the Six Mile Spruit (today known as the Hennops River), which could be made even more slippery by spreading cow dung on it, and delivered hours and hours of glorious fun and laughter.

The Six Mile Spruit, or 'the Spruit', as we fondly called it, was central to the freedom of our outdoor existence. In those days, it flowed only about twice a year. I say 'flowed' but I really mean 'flooded', as it would burst its banks after a typical Highveld cloudburst, and the resultant spate would always create a playground of gooey mud in which we played rugby and football, emerging unrecognisable at the end of the games. Not surprisingly, clothes had a short lifespan in that neck of the woods.

On the banks of the Spruit we built a football field where, practically every single day, summer or winter, matches of 'international importance' were played, and it was on the Laureston Farm field that a crop of genuinely good players honed their natural skills. A significant number later went on to play professional football in South Africa and abroad.

Afrikaans was the dominant language in Pretoria during this period (1965–1975). I estimate that Afrikaans-speaking families outnumbered their English-speaking counterparts in Valhalla by about eight to one. Even though it was 70-odd years since the end of the Anglo-Boer War (1899–1902), many of the Afrikaans-speaking kids had grandparents and great-grandparents who still had vivid personal memories of their awful treatment at the hands of British forces, or 'khakis'. From time to time, English-speakers growing up in the area unfairly bore the brunt of that lasting animosity.

In our little part of Valhalla, the very southern tip of it, we 'Rooineks' formed a gang, telling ourselves that it was for protection against the 'Dutchies'. In practice, it really meant that we could get up to more mischief as a group than we could have done as individuals.

One day my mom, ever the voice of reason in troubled times, asked me to name the members of our Rooinek gang.

'Well, that would be the Van Jaarsvelds, the Swarts, the Du Toits and the Jouberts, Mom,' I replied.

'And the Afrikaans gang members?' she asked.

'Those bloody Robinsons, Beavers, Allisons and Smiths!' I answered.

But, then again, what's in a name?

The competition between the local gangs was not fierce and never resulted in more than the odd bloody nose, blackened eye or bruised ego. However, individual feuds, though rare, did exist. I had one that extended over a few years with an Afrikaans kid named Christo. He was a year or two older than me but could never be mistaken for a street fighter by any stretch of the imagination.

The origins of the friction between us started with his father's ownership of a reasonably large peanut field, which lay adjacent to our bush playground. In great anticipation each year, we would wait for the arrival of the mobile peanut processing plant, which harvested, separated and packed the peanuts into hessian bags. Then we would strike with military precision on a daring mission across enemy lines to liberate a single 30-kilogram bag of unshelled raw nuts from behind the harvester/bagging machine. Enormously proud of our freshly acquired loot, and using the thick bush adjacent to the peanut field as cover, we would lug the heavy bag towards the Spruit and our hideaway, salivating at the thought of an endless supply of groundnuts at our disposal for at least a few weeks.

One year, in the midst of this clandestine operation and while we were crossing the open ground a short distance away from the relative safety of the Spruit, we heard a shout. There, 50 metres away, skulking behind some bushes, were Christo and his short, dumpy, red-faced and irate father.

'That are my nuts!' screeched Christo Snr. 'Bring them here, you rooinek *diewe* (thieves)!'

'Run for your lives!' shouted Brian Swart, and someone else screamed, 'The mad fucker's got a gun!'

Holding on to our loot for all we were worth, we dashed for the sanctuary of the riverine foliage, but there was suddenly a loud bang and my back and legs felt the excruciating sting of a thousand hornets.

Dramatically, one of us (I admit it may have been me) screamed, 'I'm hit!'

'We've all been hit, you silly shit!' trumpeted Tula Billett. 'The bastard just shot us with coarse-grained salt!'

Apparently, this non-lethal deterrent had been used effectively and frequently on would-be peanut liberators in the past. Explaining the welts on the back of my arms and legs to my mother as I prepared to shower that evening – 'Got attacked by a swarm of bees, Mom' – produced a disbelieving response.

But, as the sins of the father shall be visited upon the sons, I stored the events of that day in the recesses of my mind and plotted my revenge against Christo Jnr.

For more than two years all my carefully hatched plans came to naught as Christo dodged every move I made like a skilled chess master. Try as I might, I could not pin him down. At one stage I even pretended to fancy his sister and hid in the hedge with her at his front gate, hoping to trap him. But blood is thicker than water, and when she realised what I was planning, she gave me up and thwarted my dastardly scheme to wreak my revenge on her brother.

Then I got a break.

At Valhalla Primary School, where I was the head boy at the time, the principal tried to encourage good behaviour. Each week, the best-behaved student would be allowed to leave school an hour early the following Friday. Months went by before I finally managed to be chosen as BBS (best-behaved student) and was rewarded with the prized early Friday departure. Christo, who was already at high school in Voortrekkerhoogte, travelled home by bus each day, but I had never managed to reach his stop before he'd disembark and run for home, successfully dodging our inevitable confrontation time and time again.

But the extra hour that I'd earned that particular Friday gave me more than enough opportunity. I waited in delicious anticipation, hidden in the bushes behind the bus stop, for a full 30 minutes before his bus, with a squeal of brakes, stopped with a jerk and Christo disembarked. As the bus departed and Christo began the usual two-minute carefree saunter towards his home, I stepped out from my hiding place and said something like 'So, we finally meet, Dutchie!'

As quick as a flash he turned and scarpered, and I just barely managed to clip his heels with my outstretched foot, which caused him to sprawl headfirst into the dirt and devil thorns on the roadside. Cornered, he got to his feet and raised his fists while his lower lip quivered, tears only seconds away.

I suddenly realised that he was substantially bigger than me, and that should he decide to turn aggressor I might end up on the receiving end. So, to keep the initiative and him off balance, I aimed one at his nose but missed and split his lip instead.

Bellowing like a stuck pig, he broke free and hightailed it for home with me running behind him roaring invective and insults like a seasoned sailor. Occasionally I managed to connect my foot and his bum until he finally made it to his house and scurried inside like a rat diving into a sewer.

With the swagger of a man who knows he's won a long-anticipated battle against a superior-sized enemy force, I strutted my oh-so-self-satisfied way home. Revenge is so very, very sweet, or so I thought … The time to savour my hard-earned victory would not last long.

Reaching our house at 58 Viking Road a few minutes later, I decided to reward my Herculean effort with a doorstep-sized slice of French polony jammed precariously between two eye-wateringly large slices of fresh Boerstra's bread, dripping with butter and All Gold tomato sauce – a veritable feast in my part of the hood! I had just sunk my teeth into my giant sarmie when, without any warning, I was yanked out of the kitchen, lifted clear off the ground and pinned to the wall outside, my feet dangling a full six inches off the floor.

All I could see in front of me was a hand, the fingers like bunched pork sausages, balled into a fist, cocked and ready to smash my 11-year-old face to a pulp. The other hand had me by the collar and was shaking the bejesus out of my slight frame. All the while, a high-pitched porcine squeal emanating from the hand owner's fat lips tore into my ears in a screeched warning that he was going to batter the life out of me and feed my jellied remains to the pigs.

Although I was battling to focus and to breathe, I recognised the face of the peanut farmer who'd shot us with coarse-grained salt. It was Christo Snr. But then, as this bully with the contorted face stopped to draw breath before unleashing his fist, a supremely authoritative voice, the sweetest sound I'd ever heard, cut through the noise and said, calmly and clearly, 'Sir, put Stephen down or I will hit you very hard on the head with my rolling pin!'

The voice belonged to Violet Mokabudi, my second mother, the keeper of our house and my saviour on many previous occasions.

'Shut up, you black bitch!' roared the peanut farmer.

'Sir, I will not tell you again. Put Stephen down or I will hit you very hard with my rolling pin and also put pepper in your mouth for the bad words,' Violet said, her voice taking on a steely edge.

Perhaps there was some intelligence and restraint left in that anger-twisted head, or perhaps he valued his own life over mine, but after a few seconds of deep contemplation Christo Snr stopped shaking me and slowly lowered me to the ground. As my feet touched the floor I broke away and dashed to safety behind Violet's ample frame. I still remember thinking that I must have done wrong and was going to get a serious pasting from my dad when he got home, if this brute didn't get me first.

Knowing instinctively that he was living on borrowed time if he remained at our kitchen door, Christo Snr shuffled away towards his big-winged American car.

'Get your father to phone me, you fokken krimineel!' he spat.

Later that evening, when my dad got home from work, as he came in the front door he asked Violet, as was his daily bantering habit, 'What stories are we hearing today, Mrs Mokmac?' (his nickname for her). Every day, Violet would reply with her customary 'No people speaking today, sir'. But today was different, and she said ominously, 'Beeeeeeeg, beeeeeeeg trouble, sir' before spilling the beans on the events of the afternoon.

From my secret hiding place behind the rhubarb plants near the kitchen door I sat quivering like an autumn leaf as I heard Violet tell Dad her version of what had transpired. I fully expected to hear the thunderous summons 'Stephen, come here!' at any moment. But it didn't come, and I waited and waited and waited for what seemed an eternity.

Then the rhubarb leaves parted and Dad sat down on the ground right next to me. Tears immediately streamed down my petrified cheeks and I mumbled, 'I'm sorry Dad, I'm so sorry Dad.'

I remember like it was yesterday, the utterly incredulous look that came over his face as he stood up, then bent over at the waist and lifted me into his arms like a little baby, telling me over and over again that I'd done nothing wrong while he carried me into the house and laid me on the couch with a little blanket over me because I was suddenly so cold.

We waited for my mom.

She arrived home a few minutes later, and a short time after that my dad went out, 'to pay a visit to someone', Mom said.

I didn't ask any questions but Christo Snr never did lay criminal charges.

*

Our house in Viking Road was close to the short final approach of Runway 01 at AFB Swartkop. In the 1960s and 1970s, Swartkop was a particularly busy airfield, and housed Sabres, Harvards, Vampires, helicopters and transport aircraft, mainly DC-3 Dakotas and DC-4 Skymasters. Aircraft movements went on throughout the day and night. Although we as a family soon became oblivious to the noise they made, many an overnight visitor to our house complained of being unable to sleep a wink.

Over the next few years my dad established himself in a business career and was finally able to take up his lifelong dream of flying, which resulted in his qualifying for his private pilot's licence in 1970. I flew with him at every available opportunity and was consequently affected by his passion for flying. A number of my parents' friends were SAAF personnel, and while at school I was fortunate to get regular trips in a range of SAAF aircraft, including the C-130 Hercules, DC-3 Dakota and DC-4 Skymaster, which further fuelled my desire to become a pilot.

Our next-door neighbour, Major Peter Webb, a navigator on 24 Squadron Buccaneers, was killed in a low-level night sortie along the Natal coast in the early 1970s. This of course led my mom to question my oft-expressed dream of taking up flying as a career. I think that she would have preferred me to have taken a different career direction, but, being the woman she was, she never once told me this.

*

Jim Serobe was a tall and stately Shangaan warrior who'd worked for my grandparents on the family farm near Wonderboom Airport for more years than anyone could remember. As a young man, Jim had earned his warrior status by killing a lion with only a spear. He was justifiably proud of this.

From the time of our arrival from Northern Rhodesia in December 1963, one of my favourite pastimes on the farm was to sit on my haunches with Jim around his cooking fire, dipping bantam-egg-sized balls of stiff maize porridge into beef, chicken or goat stew while listening to him recount the stories of his life and absorbing his lessons on all manner of subjects. Jim could live entirely off the land, even in the peri-urban environment of the Wonderboom farm.

When asked how old he was, Jim would always reply 'One ninety ouhty one', which we came to accept as being his expression of the year of his birth, 1901 (although it could also easily have been 1891). We never quite knew for sure. He related that he had lived through the era of 'Oxpicky baggies' (Oxford bags trousers of the 1920s) and ragtime.

Jim Serobe was my other grandfather. He called me Maloui (pronounced Ma-loo-wee), which I understood to mean 'restless' or 'energetic' in Shangaan.

At one stage Jim had had seven wives and countless children, all of whom stayed at his kraal in Mozambique near the Lebombo/Ressano Garcia border post. Jim would often tell me that he preferred that the family stayed there. He was proud of his peacemaking ability when he would return home annually over the festive season, and bring a semblance of order to what he described as the chaotic situation that prevailed whenever he was away even for a short period. 'Chaotic' often meant that he would feel duty bound to kick out an errant wife or acquire a new one, or accept paternity for progeny sired by any number of locally resident contenders for their absent headman's throne. As the years went by and his prowess as a warrior chief waned, Jim gradually shed more wives than he gained.

Each time he went on leave, I looked forward to his return, as he would regale me with stories about what had happened at his traditional home and how many wives were still left, as well as matches, hatches and dispatches and all manner of interesting titbits. I came to feel that I knew each member of his family, even though I'd never really met any of them.

In 1973, he came to live with us in Valhalla, because, at the age of 72-ish, the job on the Wonderboom farm had become too much for him. But he wasn't yet ready to accept a pension and retire.

'I am still young, Maloui, my third wife just had another son,' he told me.

Dad felt it best that he was closer to us.

He didn't actually live at 58 Viking Road but rather across the road in digs on Laureston Farm, which was owned by the Billett family. There he earned his keep by turning Mrs Billett's kitchen garden into a paradise of herbs and fresh vegetables.

Jim was a man of relatively few words, but those he used were very descriptive. Shortly after being awarded stewardship of the vegetable garden, Mrs Billett called Jim and asked his opinion of the tomato bushes that she'd painstakingly nurtured and of which she was immensely proud. After years of dedicated work, the tomato patch had finally produced its first tomato, which, if the truth be told, was a rather shrivelled specimen.

'My tomatoes are producing very nicely now, don't you think, Jim?' suggested Mrs Billett.

'Dis *tamaties* (tomatoes) is fucked!' Jim retorted.

One day when Mark, Jim, my dad and I were busy building a swimming pool on our property, Dad broke wind loudly. Without interrupting the rhythm of what he was doing Jim looked up and said, sagely, 'It will rain ... I can hear the thunder.'

Each Saturday, as soon as he was paid, Jim would take a walk down to the general dealer's shop located at the little Wierda Bridge Shopping Centre nearby. Afterwards, he would invariably go to a shebeen in the bush behind the shopping centre for a pint or two of a wicked, home-brewed traditional liquor called skokiaan. Skokiaan was rumoured to contain such exotic items as rotting roadkill, insects and birds, and was fortified with battery acid. Drinking it required a very strong constitution indeed.

One Saturday afternoon, as Jim left the shebeen, he was set upon by a gang of eight young louts who were widely suspected of being complicit in a spate of recent muggings and housebreakings in the area. He was relieved of his week's supplies of maize meal, stewing meat and assorted tinned foods. Then they chased him up the road, taunting and teasing the old man as he stumbled along. Laughing loudly, they finally turned around and went back to the shebeen.

In my memory of that day, I vaguely recall Jim shuffling his way towards and into his room at Laureston Farm. He emerged just seconds later armed with his traditional fighting sticks and knobkierie and made a beeline back to the shebeen. I wish that I had been a fly on the wall to witness the events that unfolded in the ensuing five minutes.

When Jim was later escorted home by the police, they were still laughing at what they'd seen at the shebeen. They'd been summoned there after receiving a number of complaints from members of the public, who'd reported hearing blood-curdling screams and loud shouting emanating from the bush behind the Wierda Bridge Shopping Centre.

Eyewitnesses interviewed by the policemen testified that the tsotsis (louts), who'd just minutes earlier robbed Jim of his groceries, had returned to the shebeen and were sharing out their loot when an irate Jim sauntered in and ordered those not involved in the theft to move outside.

Remember that Jim was 72 years old.

The tsotsis, understandably, just ignored Jim's polite request to return his property before the shit really hit the fan, and simply continued dividing up the goods while the rest of the onlookers said a quiet prayer for the old man who was surely about to meet his maker.

It is quite possible that never before in human history were the odds against victory so heavily stacked against one man.

Undaunted, Jim waded in, fighting sticks and knobkierie flying.

For thirty seconds or so, he singlehandedly delivered a relentless barrage of chops, swipes and thrusts connecting with pinpoint accuracy to the heads, limbs and chests of his human targets. So fierce and unexpected was the assault that Jim barely had to parry a counter-blow.

Despite the ferocity of the attack, a number of the thugs managed to draw their razor-sharp knives. This only seemed to spur Jim into a greater fury, and those who wielded the blades were singled out for even more brutal punishment. Femurs, crania, radii and ribs snapped under the sustained assault and blood spattered even those spectators who had moved away from the scene of the slaughter.

In less than a minute the one-sided battle was over and on the ground lay eight tsotsis, all of them knocked senseless (or pretending to be) by this frail and seemingly harmless old man.

I am told that there was utter silence for at least a few seconds before the assembled crowd, as one, roared their approval for Jim's actions and hoisted him high upon their shoulders. Gradually Jim's eyes had begun to lose the bright red bloodlust and he'd asked to be put down. Then he calmly set about gathering up his possessions.

At this point, the police must have arrived and called for ambulances to evacuate the casualties. None of the tsotsis could walk or crawl, and so they all had to be stretchered to the waiting vehicles.

I don't know whether any of the gang ever returned to the area but I do know that Jim became a folk hero, not only with the shebeen patrons who'd witnessed his exploits but also with the police and among most, if not all, of the residents of southern Valhalla. In light of his sudden celebrity, the tragic events that unfolded just a few months later seem almost inconceivable.

Jim would always spend the December holiday with his family at his kraal in Mozambique, where he would drink copious amounts of sorghum beer with other elders from the district and eat mounds of traditional food served by the womenfolk. Typically, well into the night hours and whenever the desire took him, Jim would rise from his seat at the fireside and loudly announce his wish that one of his wives guide him to his sleeping hut, where his intention was to fulfil his husbandly mandate. In Jim's considered opinion, this would result in the chosen partner giving birth to a child just before his arrival the following Christmas, nine-month gestation period notwithstanding.

By the end of 1973 Jim was down to a solitary wife. She was a lot younger than him and, it appears, had a libido that needed more regular fulfilment than Jim could produce on the annual festive-season visit. Sometime after nightfall on New Year's Day 1974, Jim excused himself from the gathering at the fireside and went looking for his wife. Unable to find her in his sleeping hut, he went on searching and discovered her engaged in an intimate act with a far younger man from a neighbouring kraal.

Enraged, Jim immediately challenged the upstart to a duel and, no doubt buoyed by his fighting prowess just months earlier, set off to his own hut to retrieve his weapons of choice. Perhaps his new opponent had heard of the tsotsi incident and feared for his life, or perhaps Jim's reputation as a warrior provoked the less traditional reaction, but the younger man chose to wait for Jim concealed behind a bush beside the path along which Jim was returning.

As Jim passed him, the usurper leapt out of the darkness with a long-handled axe and struck three blows. The first was aimed at Jim's head and struck the old warrior on top of the forehead, slicing down and severing his optic nerves, causing immediate blindness in both eyes. The second struck him on his left forearm and simultaneously shattered the radius and humerus bones. The last blow hit him high on the back as he fell and opened a deep wound that exposed his right lung and shattered the ribs protecting it.

Jim was close to death when members of his family found him a short while later and carried him back to his kraal, expecting him to succumb at any moment.

But, ever the Shangaan warrior, Jim refused to die.

It was in this state that my frantic dad found him a few days later. Jim had failed to return to work on the appointed day, and my folks, knowing this to be unprecedented, had become concerned for his safety, prompting Dad to drive the 450 kilometres or so to Ressano Garcia in search of Jim.

Jim was carried the few kilometres to Dad's car and rushed to Kalafong Hospital in Pretoria, where the doctors performed miracles, clearing up the multiple infections and sewing up the gaping wounds. Blind and with his useless left arm in a sling, Jim was discharged three weeks later. He still walked, like a king, from the hospital entrance to a waiting minibus that took him home.

Realising that Jim's working days were over, his Shangaan and Pretoria families agreed on arrangements to ensure his comfortable retirement. Just a few short weeks later, one Saturday morning, Jim's son drove his dad to our home at 58 Viking Road.

There he sat, on the second row of the VW Kombi minibus that had brought him to us, his back ramrod-straight as ever, staring sightlessly into the distance through milky eyes as he said his goodbyes to each of us in turn.

Distraught and crying like a little child, I asked him, 'But why are you saying goodbye, *Tata* (grandfather)? Your wounds have healed and you look so well. Where are you going?' I wailed.

'Maloui, don't be sad. I am going to where I will be young again.'

Two days later, early on the Monday morning, the phone rang and Jim's eldest son quietly told us that Jim had not woken up that morning.

*

I have said before that the Six Mile Spruit played a major role in the lives of me and my friends. When it burst its banks after a rainstorm, the real fun would begin. We would play in the abundant mud, stage canoe races in handcrafted sheet-metal boats to sort out the latest neighbourhood pecking order, and wage gang warfare with air rifles and rubber pellets. From time to time waterfowl would miraculously appear and hunting expeditions with catapults, bows and pellet guns were planned and executed in intricate detail.

But the delights of the biannual floods lasted just a few short days, until the Spruit dried up again.

When I was in Standard 9, my penultimate year at Lyttelton Manor High School, one morning I was discussing with a few friends the unfortunate brevity of the periods when the Spruit actually flowed. One of them suggested that we recce the upstream course of the river to establish if some farmer wasn't perhaps damning the flow of water.

At the time, it sounded like a good idea, and four of us sectioned off parts of the river for ten kilometres downstream of the Irene Farm and set about the task of discovering who the farmer might be who was blunting our fun.

Jurgen, one of our group of four, lived in a newly built suburb called Hennopspark, through which the Spruit flowed. A few days later Jurgen reported to us that he had found a dam across the Spruit near his house. At a subsequent council of war, the four of us decided that, if the fun times along the river were to be extended, the dam simply had to go. I was tasked with approaching our neighbourhood 'scientist' with the request that he manufacture an explosive device to blow up the offending structure. I think my initial approach was quite casual in nature, and I didn't expect it to go anywhere. But then Quentin, the 'scientist', told me that he was working on a nitroglycerine-based bomb that could do the job, and things just kind of escalated from there.

When the bomb was ready, we arranged for all four of us to spend a Friday night at Jurgen's house. My job was to fetch the bomb from Quentin in the afternoon and cycle the four or so kilometres to Jurgen's home, where the others would wait for me. We planned to detonate the bomb at about midnight. Only Jurgen had seen the dam, and his description lacked a lot of detail, as we were subsequently to discover.

I collected from Quentin an odd-looking plastic jar (about the size of a 500-gram honey jar with two wires coming out of the top) filled with grey jelly, together with an old-time telephone dynamo that produced an electric current when wound rapidly, and set off for Hennopspark on my delivery bicycle.

Near the 'target' I met up with the rest of the demolition crew and we ducked into the bushes beside the river to have our first look at the object that had been spoiling our fun. We soon saw that the dam wall had long since been breached by past floods and that at least half its length had been washed away.

Unfazed by the facts and without needing much persuasion, we unanimously decided that the other half of the dam was what was impeding the main flow of the river, and that its obliteration was vital. And so the clandestine mission continued.

Following Quentin's instructions, we used a crowbar to bore a four-inch-diameter hole about six feet deep into the base of the dam. Into this we pushed the bomb, right to the end of the hole, which left only the two electrical wires protruding. We then connected the two wires from the dynamo to the bomb wires and paid out the reel of line attached to the dynamo.

I think we'd all hoped for at least 50 metres or so of separation between the bomb and our shelter, but the line supplied by Quentin extended just 20 metres. Our determination to complete the task overcame all thoughts of safety, and we reasoned that Quentin would not have provided us with a detonation controller that was too short. We led the line over the top of a large willow tree that had fallen over in the previous flood and made our shelter there.

With the device in place and ready to be detonated at the turn of the dynamo, we left the scene and went off to Jurgen's house for dinner. I am sure that Jurgen's mother knew something was up, as she spent dinnertime trying to get to the bottom of our strange behaviour. But group loyalty held firm. Her suspicions must have heightened when, after supper, instead of visiting some of the many pretty girls in the neighbourhood, we told her we planned to play Monopoly and get an early night's sleep.

At 23h30 or so we quietly slipped out of the kitchen door and made for the target, which was located about 500 metres from Jurgen's house (and, I must add, about 200 metres from the nearest building – we weren't complete idiots).

It was a calm evening and the only sounds were the rumble of cars on the nearby freeway and the odd bark of a dog in the distance. I don't recall any of us being afraid but I remember my heart racing wildly as we approached the scene of the imminent blast.

We all took cover behind the tree and began a dramatic countdown.

Five ... four ... three ... two ... one ... wind the dynamo like hell!

Nothing happened.

Try again.

Five ... four ... three ... two ... one ... wind the dynamo like hell!

Again, nothing.

'Wind it from the start,' someone whispered.

(Start winding rapidly) Five ... four ... three ...

There was a blinding flash and the earth around us lifted at least a foot in the air. A simultaneous BOOOOOOOOOOOOOOOM shattered the silence of the night.

Deafened by the enormous blast and engulfed by fumes and debris, through the haze of dust and falling leaves and branches I saw Charlie's distorted jaws mouthing a soundless 'Run!', and we were off, sprinting like cheetahs after a gazelle, only much, much, much faster.

I knew well enough not to follow the others, who were all of a similar mind, and I flew through the river, up the opposite bank and put 300 metres of terror-fuelled distance between me and the blast site in less time than it takes to say 'Shit!', which incidentally was the word I kept repeating over and over and over again for hours, days and even weeks afterwards.

On reaching a nearby road I stopped and took shelter in the shadows near a concrete wall. It seemed to take ages before I was able to breathe easily, but my heart still beat like a pneumatic drill and the fear of discovery clutched at my chest.

Figuring that anyone in the area would be making their way towards the site of the explosion, I somehow forced myself, walking stiff-legged, back towards the scene, all the while trying to pretend that I had been out on an innocent midnight stroll, in case anyone had been watching. Painstakingly, I made my circuitous way down the network of roads surrounding the blast site, trying hard to give observers the impression of someone rudely roused from their slumber by the deafening explosion.

As I approached the scene of the crime, I saw that a crowd of people had gathered at the roadside nearby. The sound of the explosion had affected my hearing, but I heard the words 'bloody terrorists' being uttered more than once.

By the time the police arrived, our little band of very sober youths had regrouped. We dusted each other off as best we could before making our way back to Jurgen's house, where we slid, like lizards, silently into bed.

'Where have you little bastards been? What have you done?' screamed Jurgen's mom, just as soon as our heads hit the pillows.

'Are you still awake, Mom?' Jurgen inquired politely.

'THE WHOLE FLIPPING WORLD IS AWAKE!' she screeched, 'Soon there will be dogs and helicopters and soldiers looking for you! Are you all mad?'

'It wasn't us!' responded an indignant Jurgen. 'We were visiting girls,' said Kevin, while Charlie, Jurgen and I nodded eagerly in agreement.

She switched the bedroom light on.

In its harsh glare, we saw that were all covered, from head to toe, in fine clay dust. Our ears, eyes, hair and clothing were a uniform pale grey. A trail of dust was clearly visible across the windowsill through which we'd gained entry after returning from our pyrotechnic foray.

'It's only a matter of time before the police come for you,' she said matter-of-factly. 'I think I will call them.'

As my throat constricted and panic threatened to make me beg and plead for mercy, Kevin, who despite this contribution never became a lawyer, said quickly: 'Jurgen is the only one who is 18. They will try him as an adult. We other three are just kids.'

We later found out that Jurgen's mom had been a young girl in occupied Holland during the Second World War and had been pressed into helping fugitives escaping from the SS. Over her dead body was her son going to be arrested and tried for terrorism while his snivelling mates walked free.

'Is anyone dead?' she asked.

'No!' came the unified answer.

'Anyone hurt?'

'No!'

'If I find that you are lying …!' she let the threat hang there.

Then, resolutely, she said, 'Quickly, off with your clothes. They need washing. And clean up the dust, every speck of it!'

I don't know whether the cops ever did call at their house or if the investigation just flummoxed the detectives, but I do know that the bond of silence between the group of four and Jurgen's mother remained unbroken until it no longer mattered.

Still, somewhere in Wierda Bridge police station archives, among the dusty old case files, is one that's probably titled 'Bomb in the Six Mile Spruit – perpetrators unknown'.

2
Joining the Air Force

Then suddenly it was 7 January 1976 and I was standing at the gates of the SAAF Gymnasium reporting for my two years of national service. When it came to doing my national service, there was only ever one choice for me: I would join the SAAF. After all, I shared my dad's love of planes and my dream was to become an airline pilot (or member of the Permanent Force). At the time, we also didn't have the funds to pay for private training as a pilot, so joining the SAAF offered another route.

In the bungalow to which I was assigned, my roommates were an eclectic cross-section of South African society. There was a Michaelhouse-educated Junior Springbok polo player, and a shepherd from the vast expanse of the northern Cape, and then there was Gavin Endres, the 'Boytjie from Benoni', who became a lifelong friend. As the Gymnasium was located barely two kilometres from my home, it wasn't long before I took to jumping over the wall in the evening and running home for supper.

A number of us had applied to become pilots, and after about three weeks we were summoned to the Gym's main gate to be briefed on our immediate future by an Air Force legend, Sergeant Major 'Bronkies' Bronkhorst. The roll call, conducted on that first evening before pilot's selection by Bronkies went something like this:

'Klopper!'

'Sar' Major!'

'Webster!'

'Sar' Major!'

'Ellis!'

'Sar' Major!'

Then ...

'Pilkington!'

'Corporal!' squeaked Pilkington.

'PILKINGTON!' screamed Bronkies.

'I'm here, Corporal!' bleated Pilkington, with an edge of frustration in his voice.

'Good shit, Pilkington!' said Bronkies, the tip of his oversized, whisky-nurtured nose twitching spasmodically. 'I was last in 1945 a fucking corporal!'

'Yes, sir, Sergeant Major!'

I don't know what happened to Pilkington after that, but the rest of us spent the next two weeks or so at the Military Medical Institute (MMI) – today the Institute for Aviation Medicine, part of the South African Military Health Service – being examined physically and mentally by a horde of interested medicos who seemed intent on finding even the slightest flaw in an applicant's make-up or character that would warrant disqualification.

For the 150 or so survivors from the original batch of about 7 500 applicants, the day finally arrived for the grand finale of the selection process – the Pilot Selection Board.

We all waited nervously outside for our turn to be called, some praying quietly, others arsing around and some just staring into space. My name was called at mid-morning, the door into the hallowed room was opened, and I was ushered inside.

I marched in, brimming with the confidence that I could convince the assembled brass that the SAAF's new Sailor Malan or Edwin Swales had arrived. Move over, Douglas Bader.

My uniform was perfectly pressed, the buttons and badges sparkled like diamonds and my shoes shone. I sat down in the plastic chair, which immediately became my throne.

The answers to their questions flew off my lips.

I was a walking, talking current affairs aficionado.

I knew who was who, what was what and how it all worked.

No doubt about it: I was their man.

After 15 minutes, they told me to piss off and try again in 12 months.

*

In the aftermath of the 1976 Pilot Selection Board's decision, I went through the full range of emotions. Disbelief was followed by anger, devastation and even embarrassment. I felt that I'd failed in what I'd set out to do and a deep depression set in.

At some point, late in the Basic Training phase at the Air Force Gymnasium, a few of my bungalow friends, including the Boytjie from Benoni, applied to become radar operators and so I listlessly went along with them. When Basic Training finished, we transferred to the Air Defence School at AFB Waterkloof for the basic radar operator's course before being posted to Devon, where the central control of the country's Northern Air Defence Sector was housed. We received more advanced training in the nuclear-bomb-proof 'gat' (hole), an underground warren of nooks and crannies filled with a range of expensive radar equipment, all programmed to utter 'wrong number, twit,' in a metallic voice whenever a student made an input error. We delighted in coaxing this robotic response at every available opportunity.

When the course ended, a few weeks later, it was time for our operational deployment and I ended up being sent to 2 Satellite Radar Station in Ellisras, 350 kilometres northwest of Pretoria. Now, in those days Ellisras (today Lephalale) was not the thriving metropolis that it is today. You reached it in three to four hours by travelling northwards on the Great North Road to Warmbaths (today Bela-Bela), then on to Nylstroom (today Modimolle), where you branched off to the left, through Vaalwater and on to Bulge River. If you reached the end of the tar road you had gone too far and needed to turn back before you fell off the edge of the world!

Coming into Ellisras from the Bulge River side, the first building you encountered was the Ellisras Hotel on the left. That was followed by 200 metres of thick bush on both sides before the Post Office appeared on the left, more thick bush and the *padkamp* (road workers' camp) on the right, more bush, a café and butchery on the left, more bush, then the high school on the left, the Air Force Base on the right. Just beyond that, the tar ended.

We arrived just as the previous intake of radar operators was preparing to depart. Our predecessors' greatest claim was that they had impregnated a number of girls from Ellisras High/Hoër School – the only coed boarding school for a radius of 200 kilometres. Consequently, the good name of the SAAF had become somewhat sullied and was not held in great esteem by the Ellisras townspeople, nor by the residents of the surrounding areas.

The first line of the briefing we received from the regimental sergeant major (RSM), one Flight Sergeant Snyman, was: 'The Ellisras Hotel are out-of-bounds to all South African Air Force peoples!'

So, we went there for a drink that evening. And every evening after that, until the farmers came in for their monthly co-op meeting a couple of weeks later …

That particular evening, we had arranged to meet in the hotel's main bar as usual after work. The first two to arrive were Klerksdorp Chris and a chap from Durban. I arrived with three others about an hour later, and as we walked in, Klerksdorp Chris flew across the pub, closely followed by his mate, as if they were darts being thrown.

About 20 local farmers were having great fun using our colleagues as projectiles. I immediately volunteered to leave the bar and fetch reinforcements but didn't get the chance to do so as I was scragged by a man-mountain quite used to throwing Brahman bulls over three-metre-high fences. He lifted all 75 kilograms of me up like a little lamb and hung me by my belt from a coat hook on the back of the door.

It is incredible how helpless and hopeless you feel when kept in suspense in this way.

I got off lightly, however, because the rest of our SAAF contingent were stripped to their undies by the farmers, then placed up on the bar counter and made to sing '*Die Stem*'. We were rescued from further embarrassment by the arrival of RSM Snyman, who had been alerted by a vigilant barman and who burst into the pub with a team of dog handlers and their faithful hounds.

As we were leaving, Klerksdorp Chris, true to his nature (I think he was a terrier of some sort in a past life), threatened to come back and teach the farmers a lesson when they next came to town. I don't think he ever succeeded in his quest or managed to find the degree of support that such a mission would have required.

So, the Ellisras Hotel was out of bounds, and no one in his right mind would go near the school for fear of being shot or castrated, or both. That meant there wasn't much nightlife. What to do?

By this time, we had ascertained that, excluding schoolgirls, there were only four or so unmarried females over 16 in the entire town. I think there may also have been a policy dictated by the Ellisras Town Fathers' Council that, in order to ensure the future of the town, these four were not to be gathered in any one place at the same time. Needless to say, we set about to defy this policy.

The Mogol River, which flows through the town, on the odd occasion formed a number of clearish pools below the low-water bridge on the northern side of town. These pools were separated by reedbeds and white sandbanks, and the site was popular for the odd braai, particularly if one could convince any local damsels to participate in the festivities.

Hard work, a lot of charm and an extraordinary amount of luck came together one memorable evening when four of us radar operators convinced all four of the available beauties to join us for drinks at the low-water bridge on the Mogol River for a braai and … whatever.

After supper, only the Boytjie proved to be possessed of the wiles to get his date to disappear quietly into the reeds with him and find a secluded pool for a skinny dip. The rest of us were left to stoke the fire, dream of what could have been and listen intently to the sounds of the night while the remaining three young ladies threw up a laager to prevent our further advances.

Unbeknown to us, the Boytjie and his partner had stripped off, got into the water, clutched each other closely enough to merge into one and were just starting to enjoy the onset of carnal pleasure when he, like a wannabe Tarzan, lifted his 'Jane' up out of the water and placed her posterior gently onto a snow-white sandbank, ostensibly to gain better traction.

Suddenly a shrill and blood-curdling scream rent the air. Jane had just come into contact with the needle-sharp reed shoots sticking out of the sandbank.

A hundred metres away, we stood up, trying to make sense of what was happening. The three uncooperative, wide-eyed and startled girls huddled together, arms around each other as the shrieking continued: 'Eina! Eina! My arse, my arse. There's something sticking in my arse!'

In a flash, one of our trio, always the quickest of thinkers in a tight situation, shouted, 'You're doing it wrong. Turn her over, Boytjie, just like the book says!'

Not even the consummate skills of the Boytjie could rekindle the carnal passions after that.

One Sunday, a few weeks after the Mogol River escapade, a three-week camper (the name for conscripts who were called up for further military service, or camps, lasting either three weeks or three months, after completing their national service) and his wife or girlfriend decided to spend the day down at the same bridge. On the way back to town in his little Nissan 1200 bakkie, the camper ran over a large black mamba. When he looked in the rear-view mirror, he couldn't see any sign of the snake and assumed that it had become entangled in his engine.

Returning to AFB Ellisras, where the rest of us were lounging around, he and his companion rapidly exited the car after parking it under a large flat-topped *kameeldoring* (camel thorn) acacia tree. With us at the time was a strange character we had nicknamed 'Grensvegter', (Border Fighter) after a character from the picture books that were popular at the time. Grensvegter had a collection of knives and weaponry that would have made his fictional namesake green with envy. He also boasted of capturing buffalo with his bare hands, and had once, it was rumoured, knocked a bull elephant lights out with a single punch. So, it was only logical that our three-week camper turn to him for help in ridding the Nissan of the lethal serpent.

Cutting a sturdy piece of bamboo from a nearby thicket, Grensvegter used a piece of stout *bloudraad* (heavy galvanised wire) to fashion a hook at the business end of the four-metre-long bamboo pole. He then told the camper to open the bonnet of the bakkie. While the camper was busy doing so, Grensvegter climbed up the *kameeldoring*. The next moment he swung down inverted, suspended from both his knees at a height of about five metres above the ground in a dead-man's-drop, at a slight angle in front of, and well above, the vehicle.

The assembled spectators, by then about 20 strong, stood mesmerised by the unfolding action and watched as Grensvegter slowly lifted the bonnet. We gasped as it revealed a large mamba entwined in the engine bay.

Getting rid of the snake should prove quite easy for one as adept as the Grensvegter, we all thought. There was thick bush close by, and once the snake was given a good reason to depart the Nissan, it would almost certainly slither to the ground and away into the bush.

Grensvegter began to prod the snake with his bamboo pole and *bloudraad* hook until, suddenly, the mamba uncoiled. But, instead of going to ground, it must have sensed that its safest and quickest escape route lay in climbing the 'branch' leading directly into the upper reaches of the tree!

Like an ultra-slow-motion scene in a movie, we saw Grensvegter's eyes grow to the size of dustbin lids and his face turn ashen.

'*Fok dit!*' roared our Grensvegter. In a flash, he let go of both the bamboo pole and the branch to which his knees were anchored, passing the mamba in mid-air and landing on his feet, all the while running at full speed.

Like a startled hadeda, Grensvegter ran to the closest armed person, snatched away his pump-action shotgun, returned to the tree and unleashed all 16 rounds at the unfortunate serpent.

Then, and only then, did Grensvegter turn to the admiring crowd and say, 'Sjoe! But that were a close one!'

After that, life returned to a semblance of normality for a short while until some operations intelligence (Ops Int) guru determined that 2 Satellite Radar Station where we all worked – the Kop, as it was locally known – was likely to be the target of a terrorist attack.

The Kop was situated on an odd, flat-topped hill about 30 kilometres east of Ellisras. We needed to understand, said the Ops Int man to his gullible audience, that the Kop had been chosen as the focal point of the Soviet/Cuban/East German onslaught against South Africa and that we, the motley gaggle of eight radar operators and eight dog handlers, were all that stood between the marauders and continental domination by the forces of communism, or words to that effect. There may or may not have been a drum roll and a clash of cymbals when his inspiring pitch ended.

Our crew included a chap from Virginia in the Orange Free State whom we all called 'Soapy'. Now, Soapy had a pathological fear of leopards and … the dark. As there were leopards resident in the bush surrounding the radar station, subjecting Soapy to any night-time activity, such as guard duty, was inviting an incident, and he didn't disappoint us.

Rather than deploy our team of radar operators in the role for which we had been trained, the powers that be decided that we would best counter the expected enemy assault by tramping around the perimeter of the radar station armed with a 7.62 mm R1 semi-automatic assault rifle and 20 rounds of live ammunition. Around and around and around we tramped, about 500 metres apart, three of us per shift interspersed with three dog handlers, hour after hour after hour.

In the northeast corner of the radar station stood the 20-metre-tall radar antenna that was used to determine the altitude of target aircraft and hence was called 'the height-finder'. It resembled a marabou stork or perhaps a Dickensian undertaker. As with almost every spooky-looking structure or tower on any military base anywhere in the world, rumour had it that a manically depressed young national serviceman had once committed suicide by hanging himself from one of the crossbeams.

To make matters even worse, for Soapy in particular, a number of the security lights on the double barbed-wire perimeter fence adjacent to the antenna were inoperative and there were consequently long shadows along the beat in that section.

At about 03h00 one morning, Soapy was making his way, at double pace, through the shadowy and badly lit height-finder segment when he became aware of something climbing onto the perimeter fence. Immediately he deduced that it was at the least a leopard or a fiendish attacker.

Taught during Basic Training to warn any attacker that they should 'Halt or I will shoot!', and to do so three times before firing, Soapy, in a bout of fear and panic, trumpeted, 'Halt or I will shoot times three!'

He then proceeded to empty all 20 rounds in his magazine into the unfortunate adolescent baboon that was having some fun by 'riding' the fence, as baboons have a habit of doing.

*

After seven months, my holding pattern at Ellisras was drawing to a close and the Pilot Selection Board for the Pupil Pilot's Course

1/77 (known as the Pupe's Course) was looming on the horizon. I left Ellisras for the last time as a national serviceman on a Friday afternoon, accompanied by a few of my radar-operating mates. The pilot selection process was to commence the following Monday morning.

And so it was, about three weeks later, that I emerged, battered and broken and in acute pain from the shortest Pilot Selection Board in history, the details of which are described in the prologue of this book. After exiting the scene of the disaster, I'd found a wooden post outside and quietly started banging my head against it. I became aware of the SAMS brigadier (the chief psychologist), who, it appeared, had followed me out of the room and was watching my antics quizzically.

'Joubert,' he said scornfully, 'please stop doing that. You will need all of your already limited faculties when you start Pupe's Course at Central Flying School Dunnottar in two months!'

And with that he turned around and went back into the room.

I stood in shocked silence for quite a while. Surely I had misheard him, or, almost certainly, I reasoned, he'd got me mixed up with someone else?

So, I resolved to tell no one until the official notification came, which was expected in a couple of weeks. Those two weeks passed agonisingly slowly as I whiled away the time playing for Strike Command in the Air Force cricket championships. The seven-wicket win that we achieved two weeks later was the first time that Strike Command had ever won the Air Force Championships.

At the prizegiving function that evening I was informed that the SAMS headshrinker who'd spoken to me outside the Selection Board two weeks earlier had been absolutely correct and that I had, amazingly, been selected for SAAF Pupil Pilot's Course 1 of 1977 (1/77). The next few weeks passed in a blur of farewell parties, good-luck parties, any-excuse-for-a-party parties and partying hard between parties.

*

The next phase of my Air Force career commenced with a day or two spent at the SAAF Gymnasium signing indemnity forms, contracts and insurance policies. There was a lot of small print, and no lawyers or parents were permitted to be on hand to offer advice to prevent exploitation. This was the price to be paid for the opportunity of being trained as a pilot in the world's second-oldest air force.

Sixty-six candidate officers reported for duty at the Central Flying School (CFS) Dunnottar, or Harvard University as it was (and still is) widely known in aviation circles. The base is located approximately five kilometres southeast of Springs. CFS was the final operational home of the North American Aviation Texan AT-6 trainer, also known as the Harvard. In southern Africa the Harvard was often nicknamed the Spamcan or Spammy, as it was said to resemble a tin of Spam.

The Harvard had been widely used as a training aircraft since the late 1930s. Although then in the twilight of its operational use, it was effective in sharpening the reflexes of fledgling pilots and demanded accurate and concise decision-making at all times. The CFS Harvards were painted silver with dayglow-orange noses, wings and tails. Few people who ever flew this lady were neutral about her. You either loved the Harvard or you hated her.

Fortunately, I fell into the former category.

Within just a few hours of our arrival at CFS, the first of many memorable events took place involving a chap who would, we had been warned by previous pupes (pupil pilots), be the bane of our lives for the duration of our time at the school: Sergeant 'Wollies' Wolmarans, the RSM's choice of dissip (disciplinarian) for the pupes. Now, Wollies was not a man of great physical stature but, like dissips through the ages, he had a voice that could turn any cocky pupe into a gibbering wreck should he attract Wollies' ire.

Our first encounter with Sergeant Wolmarans, unfortunately for him, set the tone for the next seven months. On the first morning at CFS, the 66 brand-new pupes were lounging around in the road outside the Quartermaster's store, drawing bedding one at a time. Some were smoking and others were playing with a ball when we heard the noise of an over-revving motorcycle engine and what sounded like a donkey being tortured with a red-hot poker.

Looking down the road we saw a helmetless, fuming, moustachioed apparition, mounted on his mechanical beast, hurtling towards us, foaming at the mouth and shouting loudly. The trumpeting vision of doom turned out to be Wollies on his 250 cc Honda Benly motorcycle.

It was the most laid-back character in the group who first observed, 'Who's the *doos* (plonker) on the bike?'

Wollies was travelling at a good 80 kilometres per hour when he slammed on the brakes right in front of us and tried to whip the back wheel around, as a teenager riding a bicycle on a dirt road would do. I may be wrong, but Wollies was clearly new to the art of riding a motorcycle. Had he been a little more experienced, he would have realised that there was only one possible result of his 'broad-sliding' action.

The Benly high-sided him over the handlebars and he performed a so-so somersault (four and a half out of ten, give-or-take, at any gymnastics competition) before landing in an undignified heap in the knee-high khaki bush at the edge of the road. To a man, the pupes stood and roared their approval at Wollies' spectacular gymnastic display.

Wollies never was able to intimidate our group after that.

Weeks later, Wollies caused even more hilarity with 1/77. He emerged one morning in a show of righteous indignation from behind a hangar, where he'd been hiding for God knows how long. He was determined to nab our errant group of pupes, who, in his opinion, were violating the fundamental principles of discipline by tripping each other up while marching, talking while walking and being, as a rule, generally unkempt.

What was worse, we had exacerbated his frustration by pretending that few of us could speak Afrikaans. Communicating in English was not his strong point.

As he reached us, again at speed on the same Honda Benly, he trumpeted at the top of his not inconsiderable voice, 'You clump of c**t, where are your proud?'

As we all fell about laughing uncontrollably, the last shreds of Wollies' potential to intimidate us evaporated like an early morning East Rand mist.

*

The following day, ground school started. This entailed six weeks of intensive lectures on a broad range of subjects, including crowd favourites such as the theory of aerodynamics, engines, meteorology and navigation. The standard of the lecturing and testing was high, and any exam mark below 80 per cent was deemed a failure. A mark below 85 per cent necessitated a rewrite of the relevant exam.

There were 18 subject exams at CFS Dunnottar, and another 18 exams awaited those who progressed to the second, advanced phase of the pilot training programme. Throughout the entire 20-month duration of the SAAF Pilot Wings Course, a pupe could accumulate only two failures. Failing a third exam would result in the pupe being immediately washed (expelled) from the course, never to be allowed to return.

At least once a month throughout their SAAF career, all pilots – pupes as well as those with wings – would be examined on aircraft emergency procedures and vital actions, two separate subjects, the pass mark for which was 95 per cent. Failure to achieve a pass in either of these meant you were grounded until you could achieve the desired standard.

The standard was brutally enforced and it was completely accepted by all concerned that maintenance of this level of expectation was critical to ensuring that the SAAF produced some of the best-trained military aviators in the world.

The normal attrition rate for students on an SAAF Pilot Wings Course was around 56 per cent, meaning that we could expect to lose 33 to 41 of our colleagues over the two-year course. We lost only 11, which I believe was some kind of world record.

There was a rather interesting incident during one lecture, this time on fuels, delivered by an ageing sergeant major. The sergeant major was trying to impress on us aspirant aviators the importance of the captain of an aircraft taking full responsibility for all aspects relating to the plane he was about to fly. As the sergeant major had spent the latter part of his career in charge of the CFS Dunnottar fuel depot, one could naturally expect that he would stress fuel checks by the aircraft commander as super-critical in the preflight inspection. To illustrate his point, he decided to use the example of a recent tragedy, in which a DC-4 Skymaster carrying 66 passengers and crew had crashed after take-off at Francistown, Botswana, killing all but one of those on board.

The accident inquiry had found that the crew of the Skymaster, whose four piston engines used high-octane aviation petrol (avgas), had unknowingly topped up its half-empty fuel tanks not with avgas, but rather with avtur, a jet-engine fuel made of high-quality paraffin. The substitution of avgas for avtur in the underground bunker tanks had been quite intentional on the part of the Francistown airport fuel depot manager, who'd done so in an effort to hide his illicit and cut-price sale of thousands of litres of avgas to friends, which they'd used in their motor cars. The consequence of his act of criminality was that, shortly after take-off, all four engines on the Skymaster had burst into flames and the aircraft had crashed not far from the airport.

The sergeant major said that the pilot of the Skymaster was to blame for the accident, as he had clearly not tested the fuel properly in his preflight inspection. One of our pupes, Roger 'Mounsey' Strike, immediately stood up and attempted to correct the sergeant major by telling him that the official board of inquiry had completely exonerated the DC-4's crew, as it would have been impossible during their preflight check procedures, which the crew had followed to the letter, to determine the avtur contamination.

The sergeant major, however, was insistent that the skipper of the DC-4 was ultimately responsible for the accident and angrily asked Roger, 'CO (candidate officer), what gives you the right to question my viewpoint?'

Roger replied quietly: 'Because the captain of the Skymaster was my father.'

*

After six long weeks of intensive ground school, the flying phase started with each pupe being allocated an instructor. Lieutenant Cois Maree was saddled with me.

From the very first minute, the pressure was on and the days became an endless cycle of ground school followed by lengthy preflight briefings, an hour in the air with your instructor trying to impart flying skills, followed by an inevitable 600-metre foray to the assisted ground approach (AGA) beacon as punishment for forgetting some aspect you should have remembered, then another dash to the AGA beacon just because it was there, and so on and on.

Unless a pupe was burdened with his parachute and bone dome (crash helmet) on the way to or from flying, pupes were required to run everywhere, slowing down only briefly to salute a passing officer. I was allocated to Charlie Flight, and our flight commander was the utterly fearsome Captain Trevor Schroder.

As I heard it, Captain Schroder had had a serious air accident a few years previously when the 24 Squadron Blackburn Buccaneer he was flying had entered an irrecoverable stall close to the ground, and he'd delayed ejecting from the doomed aircraft in order to make sure that his navigator crewman had safely ejected first. The momentary delay meant there was insufficient time for Schroder's parachute to deploy fully before he hit terra firma, and he'd sustained horrific injuries in the process, barely escaping with his life.

The myth doing the rounds among the pupes, no doubt instilled by Captain Schroder's fellow instructors, had it that in patching him up, the doctors had used so much steel that Schroder actually carried his own compass swing card (each aircraft has its own unique arrangement of magnetic fields and metalwork, which affect the accuracy of magnetic compass readings; the compass swing card is a reference used to correct the inherent errors).

On passing Captain Schroder early one morning on my way to the flight lines, like a good pupe I compliantly slowed to a walk, saluted him and said brightly, 'Good morning, Captain!'

He did and said nothing until I was a few metres past him, and then an eardrum-shattering roar rent the still air: 'What did you say, pupe?' (the last word being accented and spat out with all the contempt he could muster).

Turning around quickly I responded in a quaking voice, 'I ... said ... good ... morning, Captain.'

'Well, in future you will just say 'Morning, Captain!' ... and I will decide whether it is a good morning or not!'

Once the flying phase began, for the first 18 hours or so pupes flew with their instructors all the time. The intention of each was, and probably still is, to make the other vomit. The hours were all about learning the basic techniques of flying: turns going up and turns going down, power settings for this and power settings for that, stalls to the left and stalls to the right, and my personal favourite – the spin.

A spin in a conventional aircraft, if the Harvard may be described as such, was described in the old RAF manuals we used as 'an uncontrolled pitching (up and down), rolling (round and round) and yawing (left and right) motion of the airplane', all three of which happen simultaneously. Why anyone in their right mind would intentionally try to spin an aircraft while they were aboard is beyond my limited comprehension.

I know that the reason pupes learn to spin aircraft is so that instructors can teach them how to recover from this gut-wrenching, bile-inducing, terror-causing sequence. Let me play my part in pursuit of a better world for all by suggesting that it would surely be better for instructors rather to teach pupes how to avoid spinning in the first place.

Civilian pilots undergoing privately financed flying instruction condense this basic flying phase into less than half the time taken by military pilots. I am convinced that the reason for this is that national servicemen are not on hand to remove the remains of the previous night's supper from the cockpits of these aircraft. CFS, of course, had no such problem, as there were plenty of national servicemen available. The reason I later applied to fly choppers lies in the fact that a helicopter doesn't spin – well, not in the sense that a fixed-wing aircraft does.

*

Around this time, during a football match against a side from another military unit, I climbed majestically above the packed opposition defence aiming to head a ball goalwards. One defender, who must have been an athletic fellow, was competing for the same ball, but, unlike me, he decided to use his feet in a classic bicycle-kick movement.

We both missed the ball.

Unfortunately for me, however, his great big number 11, metal-studded right boot, travelling at close to light speed, connected with my upper jaw and nose. The sound of the impact, I have been reliably informed, was heard even in remote areas of the western Free State. The collision broke my nose in a couple of places, the consequences of which would ultimately have a 30-year impact on my health, and the root structures of my two front teeth took an almighty hammering too.

When I woke up the next morning, I studied my battered face through the discoloured narrow slits where my blue eyes had been.

I decided, none too cleverly, that flying trumped everything else and reported for my turn in the cockpit with my instructor, Lieutenant Maree.

By the third day after my impact with the boot, the swelling had not subsided in the least, and in fact was far worse. I was also in excruciating agony from toothache due to my bruised front gnashers, and I was trying to self-medicate by rubbing crushed extra-strength Disprin directly onto my gums. Not being possessed of effective diagnostic skills, I didn't realise that I had developed a large abscess deep in the roots of my recently traumatised pearly whites.

While flying, each time the microphone, which extended on a stainless-steel arm from the inner helmet, came into contact with either of my front teeth, which happens in the air far more often than you'd realise, I would experience such an intense burst of pain that the lights would momentarily dim. Cois Maree, in stock-standard instructor tradition and utterly ignorant of my injury, told me to 'Suck it up, chappie', and pronounced me fit to fly.

As my infection-ravaged competency, already not in the Sailor Malan class, declined further, he felt compelled to increase his use of the detachable back-seat joystick. This 'instrument of torture' was woven through the maze of tubing separating the front seat, where the pupe sat, from the rear, where the instructor was, and was used by the instructor to 'prod' a student back into line, by tapping insistently on the pupe's helmet. However, in my case, Lieutenant Maree's actions caused even more contact between my teeth and the microphone.

Something had to give, and it did.

Early one morning, after another agonising and sleepless night, a fellow student and good friend, the late 'Lang Lappies' Labuschagne, convinced me to go to a dentist and said that he would cover for me if anyone asked where I was. I know that I intended to find the resident base dentist, but when the next lucid moment arrived, I found myself outside the office of my family dentist in Pretoria, nearly 120 kilometres away.

I staggered into his consulting rooms. The receptionist immediately declared an emergency, and shortly thereafter I experienced the indescribable relief of the abscess being lanced. This action instantaneously relieved the pressure in my head, and I then felt the delight of a powerful analgesic being injected. I barely made it home to my parents' house before collapsing onto my bed and sleeping for 18 hours straight.

*

As previously stated, the first major flying hurdle on the Pupe's Course was successfully passing the 18-hour test. Once safely over this obstacle, the next stage involved pupes progressing to actually landing the aircraft.

This sounds a lot easier to do than it actually is.

All kinds of dynamic forces come into play when an aircraft gets close to the ground, and many a mishap has resulted from a momentary lapse of concentration on the part of the aircrew during that brief transition from flying like a bird to rumbling along the ground on a set of wheels like a terrestrial vehicle.

Instructors intrinsically know this, and so, at CFS, they had developed some pretty effective, though not entirely conventional, aids to help guide their students towards life-preserving success upon landing. From time to time, a fellow pupe could be seen, for days on end, carrying a set of bicycle wheels, one in each hand. The wheels accompanied the pupe 24 hours a day and nearly everyone that the pupe met would ask what had caused him to acquire these appendages. He would be required to answer that carrying bicycle wheels was the standard consequence for forgetting to extend one's undercarriage while preparing to land the Spammy. The rarity of actual landing-related accidents at CFS was a direct result of this treatment, which worked wonders for the memory and prevented a lot of 'wheels-up' returns to solid ground.

Another innovative way to correct a bad habit was for an instructor to order any pupe who was battling with height judgement on landing, to sit on the roof of the toilet block with a plastic or wooden ruler in his left hand (representing the Harvard's throttle lever), holding a broomstick (representing the joystick) in his right hand, and with his feet planted firmly on the horizontal sweeping section (representing the rudder pedals), thus simulating the primary controls used in landing the Harvard. The role of the toilet roof in this process was scientifically calculated, we were told, to be the precise height at which the Harvard 'rounded out', or levelled off, immediately before touching down. Some of the more vindictive instructors even had their pupes imitate the noise of the radial engine to add authenticity to the lesson ...

I often wondered what comments would have ensued and what delusions of grandeur would have been dashed had any of our mothers and fathers observed one of these daily gaggles comprising the Air Force's elite students, their precious sons, flying imaginary aircraft in close formation, spasmodically moving hands and feet, while making toddler-like noises, while sitting on the shithouse roof.

Nevertheless, all of this contributed to our overcoming the next obstacle, which was the one no pilot ever forgets – their first solo flight.

CFS had a long tradition in this regard. Once an instructor was satisfied that his pupe possessed sufficient ability to land the aircraft without killing himself, he would call on a more senior instructor to conduct a 'solo check', which would entail the solo check instructor's accompanying the pupe on one, two or maybe even three circuits and landings. When satisfied with the pupe's competency, the solo check instructor would tell the pupe to taxi the aircraft back to the pre-take-off holding point, near the threshold of one of the active runways (there could be up to five parallel runways in use at any one time). Upon reaching the holding point, the check pilot would get out of the rear seat, open the small baggage compartment near the tail, extract a bright red wind sock and tie this to the tail wheel of the aircraft. The check pilot's final obligation was to give the pupe a thumbs-up, releasing the virgin soloist on his first unaccompanied take-off, circuit and landing, a momentous and unforgettable event in the life of any aviator, military or civilian.

Having recovered from my face-changing incident, and after I'd accumulated a substantial number of unloggable hours flying the good ship 'Crapper', Lieutenant Maree, my long-suffering instructor, in a moment of great personal weakness, deemed me ready for my own solo check and handed me over to a more senior instructor.

An interminable while later, after I'd thumped the poor old Spammy we were flying into the ground far too many times for its health or that of the check instructor, he stumbled, ashen-faced, from the plane. The next moment he wound the wind sock around the tail wheel, made a strange gesture that I interpreted as 'Go die if you wish' but could have meant 'Cut the engine and go sell cars'. Without seeking any further clarification, I immediately opened the throttle, sped off down the runway and lifted off into a clear, windless winter sky.

It was only after I had raised the undercarriage and completed the rest of the after-take-off checks that I turned around and saw the empty rear seat and realised that I was alone. I started yelling and hooting like a lunatic, and stopped only briefly to radio the control tower and request my landing instructions. Coming in over the airfield's perimeter fence on the final approach, I thought that I'd better calm down as I was almost certainly being observed through binoculars from the tower.

Under my less-than-expert guidance (some would call it abuse) the Harvard hit the ground, bounced a few times and then settled, the speed rapidly bleeding off until I could safely turn off the runway and make my zigzagging way back to the dispersal (parking) area. I manoeuvred the aircraft into its designated parking spot on the Dunnottar flight lines, applied the brake and started the engine shutdown process.

I couldn't help noticing that a group of my fellow pupil pilots had all gathered to the port (left) side of the Harvard and were waiting for me to disembark. For more than 50 years, pupil pilots in the SAAF had followed a time-honoured procedure when welcoming home a fellow pupe who had just completed his first solo circuit, and I was about to get my once-in-a-lifetime turn.

As I got out of the cockpit and onto the left wing, willing hands removed my helmet and parachute and hoisted me high onto the

Following a long tradition, I was given a mud bath after my first solo flight.

shoulders of the cheering crowd. Without letting my feet touch the ground, they carried me 300 metres or so back to the area surrounding the pupes' crew room, stopping only occasionally for passers-by to slap my back or shake my hand.

Outside the crew room, a waist-deep pit, about a metre wide and four metres long, had been dug and filled with water, thereby creating a sizeable pool of mud. It was into this squishy mess that I, like so many who'd gone before me, was unceremoniously dumped by my colleagues.

As I write this, I still get a lump in my throat when I recall the intense emotions that flooded through me as I emerged, dripping with slime, from the glory hole. Standing there, waiting for me to exit, were all of Charlie Flight's instructors and pupes, each of whom shook my hand in heartiest congratulations despite the mud dripping from their own hands afterwards.

Now, nothing as momentous and significant in the lives of the young SAAF pupil pilots as surviving their first solo flight could go uncelebrated. So, by the time I'd finally succeeded in soloing, plans were well underway for the Pupes' Solo Party at the CFS officers' mess.

In anticipation, we pressed our step-outs, shone our buttons and buffed our shoes. We then dispersed to every corner of the surrounding towns and cities to collect our dates for the evening. My date was from my home town and her brother was about to marry the daughter of a senior SAAF officer. While waiting for her in the lounge of her home, I encountered her brother's future mother-in-law.

'What do you do?' she asked.

'I am a pupil pilot in the Air Force, ma'am. I just went solo,' I said proudly.

'My husband is a pilot too,' she stated, looking down her nose at me, clearly not expecting any reply.

'What rank do you hold?' she asked a few minutes later.

'I am a candidate officer, ma'am,' I replied brightly.

'My husband's a general!' she said, and I swear she never spoke to me again after that, not one single word.

*

After soloing, the flying intensified, with aerobatics dominating much of the time spent in the air. The Harvard, in the hands of those who know how to fly her properly, is a graceful bird and, in my humble opinion, does the best stall turn of any aircraft I know.

She will also react without warning if you are even slightly abusive to her. Many was the time when I got it slightly wrong going into an aerobatic manoeuvre and paid the immediate price of spinning out of control, losing a large amount of altitude and spending the next 30 minutes climbing back to a safe height so that I could spin out of control yet again.

The brass who make decisions on these things had decided to spare Lieutenant Maree any further punishment and allocated me instead to another instructor, Lieutenant Frikkie Knoetze, a cousin of a well-known boxer. I don't think Frikkie was a dyed-in-the-wool Harvard fan. I know this because when we landed at the end of each lesson he would say, 'I hate flying with you in this fucking aeroplane!'

I would probably not be too far off base to say that Frikkie and I enjoyed a courteous, if not particularly friendly, instructor/pupe relationship.

I had learnt quite early on that by applying an excess amount of rudder while trying to do a straight roll in a Harvard was the most effective way of making the guy in the back seat retch. To be honest, I discovered this abjectly cruel, but justifiably vengeful move purely by accident one morning following a particularly heavy instructors' pub night.

I had got quite tired of Frikkie beating me on the back of my bone dome with his joystick. In trying to avoid the wretched thing hitting me while preparing for my 60-hour test, which involved extensive aerobatics, I was attempting a straight roll (a

360-degree roll around the longitudinal axis of the Harvard) but applied an overzealous amount of rudder and was immediately rewarded with a loud groan from the rear seat. Seconds later I heard Frikkie deposit significant portions of his breakfast into a barf bag.

The game was on, and every time he used the stick thereafter, I waited only a brief period before telling him that I wanted to practise straight rolls – again and again and again!

The 60-hour test came and went and was followed by an intense period of sharpening and evaluating our aerobatic skills and introducing all manner of practical flying, including navigation and formation flying.

Before long, our days at CFS Dunnottar drew to a close, and in early October 1977 the remaining 60 or so 1/77 pupes gathered at the gates on a Monday morning. A small group of instructors had gathered to ensure our timeous departure from CFS and bid us farewell, with orders to report to Flight Training School (FTS) Langebaanweg on the West Coast.

The base was about 120 kilometres north of Cape Town and 1 500 kilometres from CFS, and we had to be there two days later … the Wednesday morning.

3

The short-lived joy of jets

Travelling in my almost-new VW Beetle 1600S Superbug for the journey to Langebaanweg was Lang Lappies Labuschagne. A sizeable group of us decided to meet that Monday night at Oranjekrag, a village near the wall of the HF Verwoerd Dam (today the Gariep Dam), about 800 kilometres from Johannesburg on the N1 highway. There we would decide on accommodation arrangements for the evening before proceeding to Cape Town on the Tuesday morning.

The first two pupes to arrive at the little hotel in Oranjekrag inquired about, and booked, accommodation for that Monday evening in a small two-bed suite overlooking the vast expanse of the dam. They were having a quiet drink looking out at the spectacular vista, minding their own business, no doubt contemplating the months ahead, when the bulk of our group arrived, galvanising the citizens of Oranjekrag into hiding their daughters, boarding up their windows and seeking shelter in their cellars. The available stocks of liquor were quickly consumed by the rampant horde of pupes.

Now, to be fair, Oranjekrag has never claimed to be the entertainment capital of the world. The lack of time-passing activities for our testosterone-fuelled group led to our resorting to drag races up and down the main street, temporarily liberating an assortment of boats to re-enact the Battle of Trafalgar, and skinny-dipping in the frigid waters of the dam. The only open restaurant/takeaway quickly ran out of stock, and groups of pupes were seen scrounging around for any source of sustenance, even if that meant knocking on the doors of residents to inquire about the availability of food.

Finally, with energy levels flagging and anticipation growing about the journey to Cape Town, which many of us would see for the first time, and which still lay some 700 kilometres away, we started casting around for somewhere to sleep and discovered that the only hotel in the area, the one where our friends had taken the only available room, was fully booked.

So, in the spirit of camaraderie for which we'd already become widely acclaimed, all 33 of our intrepid band squeezed into that two-bed suite. Each of us found a spot to lay our head down for the night. There were two pupes who slept in the bath, others who slept on top of the cupboards, still others on the tables and some found space on the floor. The little balcony was also carpeted with reposing flyers, and even the toilet provided at least one individual with a place to slumber.

Before it was even light the next morning, the early risers among us heard the sounds of the little trolley that delivered tea and coffee to hotel guests in their rooms making its way along the passage outside. A small amount of cash changed hands between an enterprising pupe and the normally underpaid tea lady, and the entire trolley, with its abundant quantity of tea, coffee and rusks, was wheeled in.

'Breakfast is served, sirs!' he trumpeted.

Everyone tucked in and devoured both the liquid and the solid contents of the trolley. Then, suitably fortified, and before we could attract the ire of the still-unaware hotel owners, our band left the hotel room and headed for the car park. As I left, I spotted an elderly couple from one of the adjoining rooms just standing in the passage staring incredulously as pupe after pupe after pupe emerged from the room.

Soon after lunchtime on the Tuesday afternoon, all 60 pupes of 1/77, as previously arranged, met in the Panorama bar of the Clifton Hotel in Cape Town. The intervening years may have clouded my memory somewhat, but I am quite sure that a plan was hatched that evening to delay our arrival at FTS Langebaanweg from the following morning, the Wednesday, to the Thursday. That would allow those of us who had never been to Cape Town to experience something of what the Mother City had to offer.

Rational thought dictated that, upon our arrival at Langebaanweg, we would be confined to base for at least a month or two, and so we unanimously agreed to make hay while the sun shone – well, for the next 24 hours at least. Nothing much happened during the next 36 hours other than a bit of drunk driving, harassment of the odd civilian and rejection of our overtures of passion by even liberally minded UCT students.

Early on Thursday morning a convoy of vehicles made its way up the West Coast road and arrived, just before 08h00, at the gates of FTS Langebaanweg. There we were greeted by a knot of scowling instructors who'd expected us the previous morning. They were in no mood to be charitable to a bunch of pupes with the growing reputation of sticking to each other like shit to a blanket and who appeared devoted to the 1/77 course motto, *Unitate Gyppoamus* (we shirk together) …

We were immediately ordered to 'inspect the perimeter fence' and, having barely had time to park our cars, set off on a ten-kilometre run. No changing into PT kit and takkies; we ran in our step-outs, comprising tunic, long-sleeved shirt, long grey trousers, tie and brilliantly shined black shoes. Not quite running gear.

The rest of the day was an unending assault of instructors screaming insults and threats, coupled with physical punishment, the combination of which was intended to bring 1/77 into line and destroy once and for all the independent spirit that burnt so fiercely in the chests of each of its members. Mercifully, at about 19h00 the instructors' screaming stopped and they went home, leaving 1/77 to contemplate its folly in daring to challenge an order.

The instructors' parting shot, delivered with great vehemence at a high decibel level, promised us that we would not see the world outside the FTS Langebaanweg gates for at least six weeks. So, after washing the day's accumulated grime from our bodies, we all got in our cars and went to the Panoramic bar in Langebaan-by-the-sea, some 20 kilometres away. Unfortunately for us, a group of FTS instructors chose to go there as well that night. Believe it or not, this was not such a coincidence as, in 1977, the Panoramic was one of only two nightspots in a radius of 50 kilometres from Langebaanweg.

As a consequence, the following day our gating was extended to eight weeks.

*

The first six weeks at FTS Langebaanweg were all about ground school and the theory of flying jet-powered aircraft. During this time, there were no flying activities and we watched our senior course, Pupil Pilot's Course 2/76, complete their training and pass their wings tests, something each and every one of us hoped passionately to do in ten months or so.

Running around the base in so-called half blues (short-sleeved shirt, long trousers and black formal shoes) became a regular, if not very enjoyable, punishment for errant behaviour, and I stacked up as many miles doing this as anyone else. We had been denied weekend passes for the duration of the ground school phase, which necessitated some creative arranging on the part of anyone who wanted to leave the base during this time.

Roll call was regularly held during these weekends by the officer on duty or his nominee. Theoretically, the roll caller could arrive at any hour, order 1/77 outside, try to get those present to stand in a semblance of order so that they could be counted and then he would call the roll by shouting the names in alphabetical order.

The means to overcome this procedure and prevent absentees from being caught called for each intended absentee to twin with a stay-at-homer, prior to his departure for the bright lights of Cape Town and its surrounding settlements. If a roll call took place, your 'twin' needed only to remember to answer for you when your name was called. This required some subterfuge on the part of the stay-at-homers, with voice-changing and constant moving around while the roll was being taken, but the tactic worked surprisingly well.

If I remember correctly, my salary at the time was about R139 per month, out of which I needed to pay a mess bill (R35), make a car hire-purchase instalment (R45), fill the car with petrol (R30) and still buy a daily packet of cigarettes and food and drink when away from the base. Toiletries and civilian clothes, as well as money to date a girl occasionally and service the car were all to come out of this stipend. It didn't take much to work out that I was going to be well short and totally broke by lunchtime on the mid-month payday.

A distant cousin of mine who lived in Somerset West stepped into the breach and made an arrangement whereby, if I could get there by about 04h30 on a Saturday or a Sunday morning, I would secure a spot on a commercial fishing boat out of Gordon's Bay catching snoek and yellowtail. As I desperately needed the additional income, I pleaded with some of the stay-at-homers to cover my tail and departed for Cape Town at the first available opportunity.

Most of the weekends during our 'imprisonment' saw my arriving at the Gordon's Bay harbour in the wee hours, changing from my uniform into more appropriate dress, and catching a few hours of sleep in the car before boarding the boat and catching snoek with hand lines until just after midday.

Upon our return to Gordon's Bay there was an old coloured gentleman who would meet the boat when we docked, and once we began unloading the catch onto the quayside, which generally attracted a crowd, he would auction off our fish. Two-thirds of the catch belonged to the skipper, and you could then choose whether to keep the share of the third that you had earned or get the old guy to auction it off as well. More often than not,

I chose the latter, which generated about R70 each time I went out, making the trip from Langebaan well worthwhile.

*

As FTS Langebaanweg ground school hurtled through its merry six-week duration, the anticipation began to rise for the next real highlight in the lives of the 1/77 pupes – the seven-day Pupe's Survival Course. This immediately followed ground school and preceded the month-long Christmas break.

The Pupe's Survival Course was to take place at a spectacularly beautiful place called Kranshoek, equidistant between Plettenberg Bay and Knysna. Kranshoek lies on one of the most impressive stretches of coastline in South Africa, slap in the middle of the Outeniqua Forest near a forestry station called Harkerville.

An SAAF C-160 Transall, a large twin-engine transport aircraft, collected our entire overall-clad 1/77 Pupe's Course from Langebaanweg and flew us to Oudtshoorn airfield. Then, using Bedford troop carriers, no doubt supplied by the local army base, we were transported by road through the Outeniqua Pass to a drop-off point located approximately 30 kilometres from Kranshoek.

At the drop-off point we were first searched for illegal contraband by the directing staff (or DSs, as they were known). Money, food and fishing equipment, in particular, were real no-no's and a thorough inspection of each 'survivor' was conducted.

We were split into 'syndicates' of 11 individuals, the leader of each of which was handed a map, and then we were all given a briefing by one of our instructors. The briefing stated that we would have about 30 minutes to make good our 'escape' before 'pursuers' would be let loose, and 'woe betide any pupe who was caught by the chasing pack', as the instructors warned. Tortures too horrible to contemplate provided the impetus for fleet-of-footedness, and as soon as we were given the order we rapidly dispersed into the forest.

We were to try to reach the 'safe haven' at Kranshoek, marked as an X on the 1:250 000 map, as soon as possible. There we were to set up our own survival shelters, made with two panels from a parachute and the abundant pine straw and brush, and to survive on plants, berries and any of the local edible wildlife unfortunate to stumble into us, for a week or so.

I know that a handful of the guys were caught on the way to Kranshoek but I cannot recall that they suffered too heavily at the hands of the interrogators, just that they were delayed for a few hours in reaching the safe haven. Somehow, I was among the first of our group to reach Kranshoek in the late afternoon. Having been on the go, unfed, since 07h00 that morning, when we'd left Langebaanweg, our thoughts immediately turned to filling our depleted stomachs.

One member of our group had the bright idea to harvest some of the abundant sea life that inhabited the rocky bay below the Kranshoek cliffs. Having collected quite a quantity of little black shellfish, which some of the more knowing chaps called *alikreukel* (giant periwinkle), we found some old five-litre paint tins, filled them with sea water, lit a fire and set the tins on the fire to boil. Then the *alikreukel* were emptied into them.

A short while later, perhaps 20 minutes or so, the *alikreukel* were ready for consumption. Vile does not begin to describe the appalling taste; marble-sized pieces of a used tractor tyre would have been infinitely more tender and tasty. If that was the preferred way to prepare the dish renowned as a 'Cape delicacy', as I have been assured it is, then South Africa has a culinary problem of epic proportions.

It slowly dawned on us that we were there to survive. This could be done successfully only by using our wits and the survival lessons learnt in the classrooms of CFS Dunnottar and FTS Langebaanweg.

So, we chose the only practical option open to us: we pooled the quite substantial amount of cash that we'd each smuggled in, in the heels of our flying boots, and dispatched three of our number to the shops in Plettenberg Bay to buy food. One of the chosen three had a relative, his brother I think, who lived in Plett. So, when he and his two companions reached the nearest telephone, they called his brother who arrived soon afterwards to pick them up.

After spending a night of great luxury at a house in Plett, the next day the intrepid survivalists went into Pick n Pay and depleted the shelves of this fine store, to the great benefit and ultimate delight of those syndicate members waiting back at Kranshoek.

Meanwhile, those of us who'd remained set about building the shelters that were to protect us from the elements for the next

On the Pupe's Survival Course - note the parachute panels in the background.

week. I learnt that a parachute has 22 panels. As there were eleven of us in each syndicate, and each syndicate was to share a single parachute, it meant two panels for each, which wasn't much.

Using the strong nylon stringers from the chute, tied to the two panels, we each fashioned a crude hammock between adjoining trees. Then we cut pine branches and large-leafed ferns, which were stacked in an A-frame structure around each hammock to keep the rain out. It is worth noting that these A-frame, tent-like structures worked superbly until it actually began to rain, which it did on the third day and hardly let up for the rest of the week.

Early the next morning, after an uncomfortable first night in the Knysna Forest, six of us descended the steep path down to the rocky Kranshoek beach, hoping to find something edible to quell the hunger pangs that were already being keenly felt. Together with the money I had managed to smuggle past the DSs in the heel of my boot, I had also managed to conceal a length of fishing line, some hooks and a sinker in the recesses of my overall.

Upon reaching the beach, I identified a promising-looking gulley, eased some shellfish off the rocks, baited a hook and launched the business end into the water of the gulley. Within a few minutes, I had landed three very, very nice blacktail (*dassies*) fish, which we cooked on a little fire and ate right there and then.

With our bellies somewhat satiated from this sumptuous meal, we all stripped naked and spent the rest of that pleasant sunny day swimming and exploring the secluded area at the base of the Kranshoek cliffs in our birthday suits. While frolicking in the raw in the heart of nature is a pleasant and liberating pursuit, overstaying one's welcome in direct sunlight on a cloudless African day will most definitely have undesirable consequences. None of us were to escape paying Mother Nature's toll for the privilege of cavorting nude in such a special place, and blisters formed in places that didn't normally see direct sunlight. The next few days were a constant and painful reminder as to why our human ancestors had invented clothing.

I caught a number of blacktail that kept us fed – and were used also as part of a ruse.

Just before leaving, one of our crew suggested that I might want to try to catch something to eat for the other starving syndicate members. A few minutes later, another three plump blacktail had ended their crustacean-crunching lives.

As we were leaving the beach at the base of the cliffs, we saw another group of our colleagues, four or five of them from one of the other syndicates, at the closed end of the beach, where they had chanced upon a fairly large snake. In the classroom, our survival lecturers had impressed upon us the palatability of catching and cooking suitably sized herpetological creatures.

The one being targeted by this group of intrepid hunters, all of whom had large stones in their hands, measured at least a metre in length and had some good meat on it. We were positioned about 50 metres from them, so our little group had a clear view of events as the hunters approached the snake.

The group was completely focused and intent on shepherding the snake into a corner with the intention of killing, skinning, cooking and eating it. Now, a metre-long snake, weighing a maximum of 1.5 kilograms, poisonous or not, should not have been a contest for five starving pupil pilots armed with human-head-sized boulders.

And no contest it proved to be.

At the last possible moment, the serpent realised that it was cornered and heading for disaster. The next moment the snake suddenly turned, reared up, hissed once and moved, quite quickly I admit, towards the group of brave marauding hunters.

Shrieks and screams, the volume and shrillness of which I could never have imagined, rent the air. In the blink of an eye the well-organised hunters were fleeing headlong down the rock-strewn beach, weapons and poise discarded, pursued, but for only a short while, by the pissed-off serpent before it spotted a gap in the thick coastal bush and slithered quickly away to safety.

'I wasn't really that flipping hungry!' I heard one guy say, and his mates all nodded sagely in agreement.

After that undoubted highlight of the first, full Kranshoek day, the five of us trudged slowly up the steep path and back to our survivors' campsite. On the way, we happened to pass a middle-aged civilian couple who had just finished enjoying a late afternoon braai at the Kranshoek picnic site at the top of the cliffs.

Acting like malnourished vagrants, which we probably resembled, three of our group launched themselves into a bush after we saw one of the picnickers throw a well-chewed lamb cutlet bone into it.

'*Bliksem, vrou,*' said the middle-aged man to his rotund wife, '*wie is die donders wat so bleddie honger voorkom?*' (Good gracious, dear, who are these hooligans that look so hungry?)

'We were dropped here a few weeks ago just in our overalls and told to survive!' exclaimed Colin Brits, who could always feign a sincere expression when required. 'We are Air Force student pilots abandoned here and we don't know when or if they are coming to fetch us!' he wailed.

'It's bullshit that they are treating our boys so badly!' said the Oom. 'I have a son who is doing his national service, and although he gets a lot of kak, they never tried to starve him! Wait here. We will be back soon.'

He and his wife then drove off, returning an hour or so later with ten loaves of fresh bread and five large cans of apricot jam, which they gave to us. Vowing to return the next weekend to check up on our welfare, they drove off to their home in Klein Brak River.

Armed with this bounty, we walked back into our syndicate's camp.

'Come and look what we got!' we crowed.

The only response to our exciting news was a two-minute chorus of belching, burping and farting, and then finally one of our mates said, 'We're full', before resuming an ultra-relaxed pose in his hammock.

It seems that while we were out for our day at the beach, the three syndicate members who had spent the night in Plett had returned from their shopping spree with a veritable truckload of assorted food, drink and delicacies, more than enough to keep us well fed and happy for the entire week and beyond. They'd hidden the bounty in a nearby cave, to be consumed at leisure. So nice was the cave, in fact, that three of them slept there as well.

By the next morning, the three fish I'd caught the previous day were still completely untouched, but it had also become apparent that news of my angling prowess had reached the ears of the DSs, and a couple of them soon arrived at our site in a Land Rover to query the information.

'Where did you get the fishing tackle?'

'Found it in the rocks!'

'Where did you catch those fish?'

'In the sea.'

'We have a helicopter to take us fishing anywhere we want on this stretch of coastline and we haven't caught anything like that yet!'

'He actually caught nine blacktail yesterday and he only fished for about an hour! That's why we are all so well fed,' gloated a teammate.

'Those are just the smaller ones,' said another.

'Fucking jammy pupe!' said the DS and they sped off in the Landy to look for better fishing spots.

One of the syndicate members suggested that I carry the three fish around with me wherever I went to give any extra-syndicate observers the impression that we were 'eating so well because I was catching so well', to use an adaptation of the famous Farmer Brown chicken advertisement. This I did until the smell became so dire a few days later that I discarded the fish down a deep ravine, in the process probably destroying four or five species of critically endangered fauna and flora. (Kranshoek and its surrounds is, after all, a highly ecologically sensitive environment.)

During this period, each time a member of the DS saw me, I waved the three fish in the air and told them that I'd just caught them and pointed vaguely in the direction of a different spot on the rugged coastline below. A short while later, a gang of DSs would scramble down the precipitous paths to the position I'd indicated and flog the water with their sophisticated fishing gear for the next few hours, becoming increasingly frustrated as cast after cast produced little, if anything, in the way of edible fish.

These tiny victories made the time pass a little quicker and made life that much more palatable under the circumstances. Before long, the final morning on survival dawned and late in the morning we were all summoned to the DSs' camp, where a sumptuous feast of steaks and beer awaited.

*

With the three-week Christmas break looming, spirits were high indeed. Added to this was an achievement by 1/77 which, to the best of my knowledge, no Pupe's Course prior to ours, nor subsequently, had/has ever accomplished.

It is generally accepted that the 'wash rate', which quantifies the percentage of pupes who are unceremoniously booted off the Pupe's Course for failing to achieve the minimum academic, physical or flying standards, was about 50 per cent after FTS Langebaanweg's ground school phase. This embodies the reality that not everyone is destined to become a qualified SAAF pilot. In the case of Pupil Pilot's Course 1/77, our wash rate was less than 15 per cent at the close of the ground school phase at Langebaan and would reach only 17 per cent by the time the survivors received their pilot's wings!

The consequence of this achievement was that FTS Langebaanweg could not accommodate all of us for the flying phase on Impala jet trainers, which was to start in January following the holiday. So, 11 of our number, who would go on to be informally known as '11 Fighter Wing', would not return to Langebaan after the holiday but would instead go back to CFS Dunnottar and complete their Wings Course on Harvards.

Christmas and New Year came and went. After three weeks of waking up late, chasing after Pretoria's most attractive lasses and drinking large amounts of beer and wine, it was time to make the long trek back to the Cape West Coast. It was time to start flying the Aermacchi MB-326, a two-seat jet trainer known in South Africa as the Impala Mk 1.

In SAAF flying training, two pupes were normally allocated to a single instructor. On a weekly rotation, one pupe would fly in the morning while the other would do ground school, and they would swap around in the afternoon. Our instructor was a career jet pilot by the name of Lieutenant John Bain.

Let me say right upfront that I did not enjoy flying the Impala. At the time, I would have really struggled to articulate my reasons, and it was only much later in my life that I realised what the primary cause may well have been.

When I was about seven or eight years old I visited the Cango Caves near Oudtshoorn with my family. Climbing through the caves was quite an adventure, and when a group broke off to climb through the dangerous-sounding Devil's Chimney, I resisted the advice of both my parents and joined them. I recall going through a narrow tunnel of perhaps ten or so metres. Ahead of me was a quite large lady. About three-quarters of the way through the tunnel her ample posterior became wedged in the confined space and she began to panic. Behind me was another quite sizeable lady, and when the instruction was shouted down the tunnel to reverse out the way we had come, she too had a lot of difficulty in manoeuvring her butt and also became stuck. Ahead of me and behind me were obstacles I could not hope to get around, and to make matters worse both ladies began sobbing hysterically. Like the meat in a sandwich, I had no space to move.

Although my incarceration lasted probably no more than 20 minutes or so, it seemed like days before I was extricated and reunited with my understandably concerned parents. When I dredge up that memory, I still feel that claustrophobic sense of hopelessness and helplessness, probably more intensely now than I did then.

The Cango Caves experience left me with moderate to severe claustrophobia, and so being strapped tightly into the Impala's Martin-Baker ejection seat, which drastically restricts one's range of movement for quite logical and understandable safety reasons, caused me intense discomfort, which grew into an aversion to the aircraft that the Impala really did not deserve.

For the first few hours on the Impala, Lieutenant Bain and the Pupe's Course syllabus dictated that we stay in the immediate environs of the airfield, honing take-off and landing skills. There was consequently no need to climb to any great altitude. Then, when he deemed I'd got the hang of landing the aircraft, we left the circuit and climbed up to 25 000 feet (7 620 metres) or so and did a few aerobatics, which to me seemed a lot more straightforward in the Impala than in the Spammy, because there were no noticeable gyroscopic or torque influences and the available power seemed endless. After a pleasant 45 minutes or so in the FTS Langebaanweg General Flying Area, it was time for us to return to the base and we began our relatively (compared to the Harvard) rapid descent.

Passing through 16 000 feet (4 875 metres) I suddenly became aware of the first twinges that something wasn't quite right inside my head. Something tangible and physical was seriously, seriously wrong. What started as an uncomfortable twinge, not unlike a light prick with a pin on my cheekbone, rapidly grew into an indescribable agony stretching across my forehead, into my ears and inside the recesses of my slightly chubby cheeks. And the pain just built and built and built.

In the few seconds that followed the onset of the attack, I completely lost my vision and with it any degree of control of the aircraft. I tried to push the intercom button on the stick to tell my instructor, seated in the rear seat, what was going on, but I imagine that all he heard coming out of my mouth was gibberish.

The volumes of blood and air in my head rocketed, the pressures thus created increased exponentially, and I truly felt that my head was about to explode. Understand that while this was going on, my head was encased in a tight-fitting flying helmet and my face covered by an oxygen mask, both of which were rapidly filling up with assorted bodily fluids (as in blood) being secreted through every available cranial orifice.

Lieutenant Bain, in the rear seat, realising that something was terribly wrong, said, 'I've got it' and immediately took over control of the Impala and stopped the headlong descent. I can vaguely recall a lot of radio chatter between him and the control tower, and then a slight improvement in the 'head pressure' situation as he initiated a gentle climb, under advice from a specialist aviation doctor who'd been summoned to the control tower. It seemed to me that it took a lifetime for the aircraft to slowly descend and land, and I only really began to regain my faculties when the ground crew opened the cockpit, the medical staff eased me out of the bang seat, and the doc took me to the Langebaanweg sickbay for further treatment and evaluation.

Surprisingly, once they'd cleaned the gore and other detritus from my facial cavities and given me a strong pain tablet or two, I was able to stand without falling over. Under strict written orders (my hearing was rather impaired, as you can imagine) to return to the sickbay the following morning for tests – with further tests planned at 2 Military Hospital in Cape Town – I self-propelled myself back to my room in the officers' mess a short distance away.

Comrades-in-arms are a special breed of men, and it is well beyond my command of the English language to try to describe the strength of the bonds that evolve between chaps who have endured or experienced the life-changing camaraderie of a Pupe's Course. The fellows on Pupil Pilot's Course 1/77 were the very best of the best.

When I look back on that horrible day in January 1978, I remember sitting dejectedly on the edge of my bed for hours, contemplating my prospects. I was thoroughly confused by what had happened and so absorbed in my own misery that I can only vaguely recall the visits to my door of my course mates, each quietly offering their sympathies, or so I surmise.

Thinking about it now, I don't know why their utterings were so subdued.

After all, I was deaf.

Finally, I curled up in a little ball on my bed, turned away from the door and closed my eyes, hoping that I'd soon wake up and it would have all been a nightmare.

At some point that evening, as I wallowed in my misery, tossing and turning and regularly changing the blood-soaked towels with which I'd covered my pillow, a course mate roused me and told me that there was someone on the telephone for me in the hallway near to my room. Obviously, this was long before cellphones, and we had to make do with public telephones (tickey boxes).

By then my hearing had improved sufficiently for me to make my way gingerly to the phone and say 'Hello' into the mouthpiece.

Seemingly from a long, long way away and down an extraordinarily long tunnel I heard my mother say, 'Son, what's wrong?' and my eyes suddenly became misty.

I had always had a special relationship with my mom. She knew instinctively when I needed her close and, conversely, when to let me bang my own head into the walls I so often created (and still do). I would normally go for months without talking to her, particularly when I was away from home base in Pretoria, but she always, and I mean always, knew when to call and when I desperately needed her quiet guidance and her maternal embrace.

I could hardly hear anything she said that night, but the sheer comfort of knowing she was connected to me, albeit by a telephone line, remains one of my most treasured memories of her.

*

The days that followed were a jumble of tests, prods and probes with little worthwhile outcome other than the expert deductions of the specialists diagnosing the causes of the '16 000 AGL (above ground level) incident', as it became known. They were of the considered opinion that an unknown impediment had prevented the sinus cavities in both my forehead and my cheekbones from equalising their internal air pressures during the rapid descent. Furthermore, it appeared that my Eustachian tubes, which connect the middle ear to the throat, had also been blocked, causing a similar pressure differential between the inner and outer ears and causing both eardrums to rupture.

Either way, I was forthwith grounded and would be sent to 1 Military Hospital in Pretoria for further tests. I left for Pretoria the next day. I cannot recall the name of the ear, nose and throat (ENT) specialist who examined me at 1 Mil but he was definitely not chosen for his sparkling bedside manner nor, it turned out, for his diagnostic or surgical skills.

In the 'discovery' part of his examination, I had told him that, six months or so before, I had had my nose broken while playing soccer, and also how my dental work had been totally messed up during an ill-fated cricket match, during which I had been struck in the face.

'Aha,' said the ENT specialist. 'It is my opinion that the combination of these two incidents caused bone shrapnel to lodge in your nasal cavities at the entrance to your sinuses and basically plug them tight, preventing the degree of equalisation required when descending rapidly from high altitude in a non-pressurised jet, like the Impala.'

He proceeded to hold my head in a vice-like grip and thrust an implement that looked like a stainless-steel knitting needle, the tip covered in spirit-dipped cotton wool, up my nose, into my throat and almost out through my bum.

I squealed like a suckling pig about to be dispatched for the Sunday roast.

'Aha! You see, there is an obstruction!' he trumpeted. 'We will conduct a sub-mucus resection with an intra-nasal ethmoidectomy. SME/INE for short!' The expectant glee dripped from his voice.

He offered no opinion as to the reasons for the blocked Eustachian tubes, however. Had he carefully considered this aspect, and referred me to someone with skills in that field, it might well have prevented a lifetime of sinus problems for me and even helped me make a full recovery.

Nevertheless, at the end of his cursory five-minute inspection, the esteemed surgeon pronounced that I was to report back to 1 Mil the following day for surgery to remove the bone shrapnel. Being a compliant young soldier (at least in this context), I didn't argue and presented myself for the suggested butchery the following day.

The pre-med administered in those days had quite a number of unwanted side-effects, and its primary effect on me was to loosen my tongue even further than normal (which is saying something, believe me). As I lay on the stretcher waiting to be taken into theatre, the anaesthetist asked me if I had any questions. I replied: 'Just one. Ask Dr Mengele why my ears are also fucked?'

Little did I know that the Mutilator of 1 Mil was standing right behind me.

I woke up in a distressed state a few hours later with my hands tied to the sides of my bed to prevent me from again pulling the metres-long gauze plugs out of my nostrils. I felt claustrophobic, and it took a number of the other patients in the ward to calm me down. The chap in the bed next to mine told me that the nurses were all angry with me, and were ignoring me flat as I had been extremely disparaging of them while they were putting me back in my bed after the op. Of course, it was a side-effect of the anaesthetic drugs.

Discharged three days later, I spent a week recuperating at home (with a night back in hospital after a bout of nasal haemorrhaging). Suitably repaired, or so I thought, I drove the 1 500 kilometres back to FTS Langebaanweg in my VW Beetle.

It was another week or so before I was given the all clear to get into an Imp again. Off we went, me and another instructor, for a low-level flight down the Atlantic coastline from Langebaan to AFB Ysterplaat in Cape Town, where we landed and had a cold drink.

The plan for the return flight was for us to take off from Ysterplaat, climb to 25 000 feet (7 620 metres) and do the normal (relatively rapid) descent before landing at Langebaanweg. It was a beautiful day as we climbed out over the Cedarberg, with the expanse of the western Cape spread out below us as far as the eye could see.

'Are you ready for the descent?' asked the chap in the rear seat, all too soon.

'Sure, sir,' I replied, and he reduced power and we started losing altitude.

I watched the altimeter wind down ... 24 000 ... 23 000 ... 22 000 ... 20 000 ... 17 000 ... 16 000 ... I was starting to smile broadly as we approached 14 000 and I still felt great when, like a switch being activated, the acute agony, the muck, the blood and the mucus struck again, filling every available nook and cranny in my head, my helmet and my oxygen mask.

When we finally landed at Langebaan after a gentle descent, it was clear that the likelihood of my flying again was exceedingly small. The despair I felt that evening is palpable to this day.

Fortunately, my guardian angel got involved again.

While the powers that be decided what to do with me, I was posted to SAAF Training Command Headquarters in Pretoria. At Training Command, my job entailed meeting with and advising aspirant pupil pilots, most of whom were still at school, on the conditions they were likely to encounter during the pilot selection process, medical examination and selection board, as well as on the course itself.

Soon after taking up my new appointment, I was contacted by a Dr Van der Laan from the MMI in Pretoria. He had become aware of my predicament and asked to see me for an evaluation.

Dr Van der Laan was known far and wide by everyone who'd ever been through a medical exam at the MMI, which was where aspirant SAAF pilots began the pilot selection process by undergoing psychological testing, a thorough medical examination and psychological and vocational evaluation. The MMI was also where all Pretoria-based aircrew underwent their annual medical assessments and where aviation-medicine-related issues were tackled and solutions to problems developed. Dr Van der Laan was a leading specialist in aviation medicine, and many pilots, both military and civilian, owe their careers to the insight, skill and intellect of this remarkable officer. I am honoured to be one of those.

After a detailed recording of exactly what had happened to me, Dr Van der Laan seemed quite certain that the 'shrapnel', while possibly being a contributory factor, was by no means the cause of my problems, and he set about getting to the bottom of the matter. This involved conducting testing whereby I was subjected to 15 or so allergenic agents. These were injected just under the skin on one arm, with the same 15 agents being rubbed into small incisions in the skin of the other arm.

Within minutes, hives were breaking out all over my body, mucus was streaming from my nose and eyes, and sensitive areas became inflamed. Mercifully, heavy doses of anti-histamines were administered and someone found me a bed in the Institute. I slept for the next 24 hours.

Dr Van der Laan discovered that I was hyper-allergic to dust, grass and feathers. All these allergens abounded in the environs of Langebaanweg in particular, but also throughout southern Africa. The treatment regimen he developed for me involved my having to undergo twice-weekly injections thereafter of a substance he concocted in a laboratory. It turned out to be a successful way to desensitise me to the agents to which I had developed such a strong allergic reaction. The measures quickly took effect, for which I am eternally grateful.

A month or two later, and without actually openly castigating the 'work' done by the Mutilator of 1 Mil, Dr Van der Laan muttered under his breath about how the Mutilator appeared to have done little to alleviate my allergy problem. On the contrary, it seems that the SMR/INE had created quite a lot of scarring to, and permanent swelling of, the mucus membranes in my nose.

'Still,' said the good doctor after working his desensitisation magic on me for a few weeks, 'I believe that I can reduce the swelling of the mycosa sufficiently to enable you to return to flying training, albeit that unpressurised jet flying may not be on the cards for you.'

*

After just a few more weeks at Training Command, my grounding was lifted and I was delighted to be returned to flying training. I did not go back to FTS Langebaanweg and the Imps, but rather was sent to CFS Dunnottar and the Harvards that I enjoyed so much.

I was joined there by another candidate officer (CO) by the name of Brian King. I cannot remember the circumstances surrounding his posting to Dunnottar as my fellow pupe, but we were to complete our wings training there on Harvards, just as '11 Fighter Wing' had recently done. I was delighted, and sailed blissfully through the months that followed, with flying in the mornings and ground school in the afternoons.

One of my instructors during that second phase of my pilot training at Dunnottar was Major Denzil White, an immensely skilled chopper pilot who became famous for his legendary exploits during his later tenure as a Puma pilot at AFB Durban. I was told that he broke many hearts in the greater Durban area when he finally tied the knot. One day, while we were cruising along on a long navigation exercise somewhere over the Eastern Transvaal Highveld, out of the blue and without any prior warning or relevance, Major White's microphone clicked on and he said to me, 'Joubert, when you get married some day for the first time, for God's sake, marry for money!' Then his mic clicked off.

Nothing else was said for the rest of the flight.

Like most young men of that time, I failed to heed this invaluable advice.

Days turned into weeks and weeks into months, and my final wings test was approaching fast.

To relieve the stresses of flying training, I had taken to leaving the base (without permission, so AWOL) each Wednesday evening at about 18h30 and travelling to Pretoria to play tenpin bowling in a formal league team that comprised five players – me, two gay hairdressers and two of the most striking red-headed ladies that I have ever seen. With time, my luck held again and one of the ladies deigned to go out with me, and for a short while we became something of an item.

So, for a period I would leave the base at the end of the day, grab a quick bite to eat, start the league at 20h30, finish playing at about 23h30, join the rest of my team in partying up a storm, and then return to Dunnottar, bleary-eyed, sleep-deprived and invariably moderately inebriated, at around 05h30 in the morning.

On the third Thursday morning after the start of my Wednesday-night escapades, and halfway through a torturous hour of my delivering gut-churning, ball-in-the-corner, pretend aerobatics, Major White's mic clicked on and he said, 'What the fuck do you do on Wednesday nights?'

'I beg your pardon, Major, but what do you mean?' I muttered lamely.

'I asked what the fuck you do on Wednesday evenings, because every Thursday lately you have been flying like a prick!' he shouted.

No, I'm wrong. Major White never, ever shouted. He was too cool for that. He might have raised his voice slightly but he didn't shout.

There was probably no other instructor in the world with whom I would have taken the chance to be that honest, but Denzil was like no other instructor and so I told him about the bowling, the partying and the redhead.

Then I held my breath.

Five minutes passed, and maybe another five, and then his mic clicked on again.

'We'll fly only on Thursday afternoons in future, OK?' said the good major.

*

The days and months leading up to my final wings test passed in a blur, and suddenly my extended struggle to earn those coveted silver wings on my chest was over.

Despite all the ups and downs, the broken noses, the despair at being grounded and the other curveballs thrown at me, I'd somehow met all the standards and could now proudly state, to all who would listen, that I was a qualified SAAF pilot. In passing the final test, I became the 55th member of Pupil Pilot's Course 1/77 to earn my wings.

With there being only two of us on our 'sub-course', the post-wings-test celebrations were somewhat muted, and were confined to a few drinks in the Dunnos pub with our instructors. Brian and I had done our wings tests slap-bang between the twice-yearly Pilot's Wings parades, which were usually grand affairs in front of sizeable crowds of well-wishers and all manner of smartly turned-out soldiers marching in an honour guard with shouted orders and bands and all the pomp and ceremony befitting such a prestigious celebration. In our case, it was unclear as to when we would actually receive the wings themselves from the SAAF hierarchy.

That left us in limbo. We were now qualified SAAF pilots, but as we hadn't yet formally been presented with wings we couldn't be used in any flying role that mattered. So, we were temporarily posted to the CFS Dunnottar Station Flight. This was where young, newly qualified pilots, also known as 'station sluts', or *stasieslette* in Afrikaans (singular: *stasieslet*), tested the Harvard aircraft after minor repairs had been conducted at the base itself. They 'swung' magnetic compasses to enhance their accuracy, flew ad hoc flights – for example, to convey replacement parts to unserviceable aircraft stuck at faraway airfields – and conducted formal test flights at Fields Aviation at Rand Airport near Johannesburg, where SAAF Harvards underwent major overhaul and repair.

The temporary jobs assigned to Brian and me involved being the onboard scribes during these tests. We had to record in writing on the official paperwork provided, all the relevant data being passed to us verbally by the station sluts conducting the tests.

The formal tests at Rand Airport could sometimes be stressful events for the young pilots who had to conduct them. They were not qualified test pilots, nor did they have any great experience of test flying, but they were nevertheless given the responsibility for evaluating and ultimately signing off the newly repaired/serviced Harvards as being airworthy and usable to train the next crop of SAAF aviators at CFS Dunnottar.

Lengthy preflight checks were carried out, using a detailed checklist, and literally every nut and bolt was carefully inspected by the designated station slut before taking the Harvard into the air for the flying section of the test. Nevertheless, incidents still occurred. One day, one of the station pilots, having taken all due care with the preflight inspection, went hurtling down the runway under full power. When he reached take-off speed and gently eased the stick back to get airborne, the aircraft seemed to grip the earth even harder than before and refused to fly. Fortunately for the quick-thinking young aviator, he realised that something was very wrong. Mentally calculating that there was enough runway left to abort take-off and stop the Harvard before it crashed into the boundary fence, he immediately closed the throttle, slammed on the brakes and brought the aircraft to a shuddering standstill.

In this particular case, it seems that the control cables, which run through a number of pulleys connecting the joystick in the cockpit to the elevator on the tailplane, had somehow been switched around on one of the pulleys, in error. Instead of the nose of the aircraft pitching up when the stick was pulled back, it did the opposite and pitched the nose downwards.

The only thing that prevented a tragic and almost certainly fatal accident from happening that day, was that a wide-awake young SAAF pilot was at the controls. Perhaps that is the most fitting testimony that I can give to the excellence of the Wings Course training given to SAAF pilots.

In the flight tests themselves, every imaginable aerobatic manoeuvre was carefully carried out to ensure that the aircraft was operating within its design parameters. The last stage of the test flight was my least favourite and involved spinning the aircraft from a great height, with the pilot holding it in the spin, to complete a full eight rolling, pitching and yawing revolutions before recovery was initiated. This exercise was guaranteed to expose any latent defect resulting from the major service, and naturally the 'scribing' was done after the aircraft had (hopefully) returned to straight-and-level flight after the extended spin. This type of flying was quite obviously nerve-jangling and not for the faint of heart.

During this period, about 40 Harvards went to Durban for the weekend, each carrying a crew of two under the guise of a 'long navigation exercise'. Thirty-eight of the Harvards were crewed by trainee instructors and their respective tutors. I flew in one of the remaining aircraft with one of the *stasieslette*.

All the aircraft headed for a place called Tugela Ferry in the Natal hinterland. On reaching Tugela Ferry, the idea was to descend quickly to ground level and then fly down the Tugela River valley at low level, turn 90 degrees to starboard (right) upon reaching Tugela Mouth on the Indian Ocean coast, and proceed, still at low level, along the North Coast of Natal to a landing at AFB Durban.

The *stasieslet* and I carried out the instructions to the letter and arrived unscathed at the mouth of the Tugela River, where we turned south in the direction of Durban. To pass the time, I related to him that I had family who had lived at Shaka's Rock for a number of years, and also that this was the legendary spot from which Zulu warriors who had been defeated in battle would be cast to their deaths on the jagged rocks below.

The 20-metre-high rock stands at the northern entrance to a small inlet called Thompson's Bay. I knew the place well, having spent many hours fruitlessly fishing from its heights. Thompson's Bay was also where a significant number of local beauties spent time sunbathing, occasionally topless, in relative seclusion from prying eyes. Thus was the groundwork laid for a close aerial inspection of the beach at Thompson's Bay (and any of its attractive occupants) as we flew by. It was, after all, directly on our route to AFB Durban.

Even though the Harvard is not the fastest aircraft on earth, it still gets along at quite a fair clip, and we rapidly approached Thompson's Bay, passing the Salt Rock and Shaka's Rock hotels. A few seconds later, Shaka's Rock was abeam on the starboard side. So mesmerised were we with spotting gorgeous tanners on the beach that it was only at the very last second that we saw the kite-fisherman standing atop Shaka's Rock. I recall clearly that his mouth was agape at an almost impossible angle and his posture remarkably aggressive.

'What's that idiot so upset about?' I muttered under my breath a split second before I observed, in what seemed like slow motion, how his large rod and reel were torn from his hand and catapulted into the air between him and our airborne chariot.

'I think that oke just lost his tackle!' said the *stasieslet*, somewhat redundantly.

Realising that we might just be in a bit of trouble, we headed for Durban as fast as the Harvard could carry us.

Ten minutes later we landed on Runway 23 at Louis Botha International Airport (now no longer operational), from where we would taxi to AFB Durban. Louis Botha had an area on a taxiway near the southern end of Runway 23 where an aircraft the size of a Harvard was invisible to anyone in the civilian control tower or anywhere on AFB Durban.

A good *stasieslet*, and the one I was flying with was one of the best, would know important information like the vantage points from which an arriving Harvard could be seen and where not. So, as we turned off quite a long way down Runway 23 and entered the taxiway going northeast back towards the parking area at AFB Durban, we disappeared from the line of sight of any interested observer in the tower or at the Air Force base.

As we did, the *stasieslet* slowed the Harvard right down to a crawl and asked me to jump out of the aircraft, still with my parachute strapped to my backside, and run along next to the plane, removing any traces of fishing line that might still be attached to our tail. This took just a few seconds, and I jumped back into my seat and we continued taxiing, at increased speed, to the AFB Durban parking area.

Before the chocks were even in, a delegation of officers arrived and immediately demanded to know why we had been flying so low and so dangerously along the coastline north of Durban.

'Not us!' we echoed simultaneously, looks of shock, horror and incredulity etched on our unlined and innocent faces. 'We would never break the rules!'

But, within seconds, there was a triumphant 'Aha!' from one of the technical officers (TOs) inspecting our Harvard. The other members of the rapidly assembled inspection party gathered around the gleeful TO, who was standing observing our tailplane.

'Look!' he said pointing at the horizontal stabiliser, where he had discovered evidence of something that had obviously impacted the elevator's leading edge at high speed and gouged shallow furrows in its paintwork (as might be caused by heavy fishing line coming into contact with a Harvard flying at 150 knots, or about 275 kph).

'Deny everything!' whispered the *stasieslet* to me through clenched teeth.

Just then there was a disturbance as the Harvard that had followed five minutes behind us arrived.

'It's probably them. They always fly too low,' said the *stasieslet*, loudly enough for the welcoming committee to hear.

'Bah!' responded their obvious leader, a guy with a massive handlebar moustache, but then, a little tentatively, and to cover all bases, he dispatched another of his TOs to scrutinise the arriving Harvard, just to make sure.

As it happened, that Harvard also had gouge marks on its tail.

And so did all 40 Harvards that arrived in Durban that day.

It seems that flying too low and too close to the beach was common practice among Harvard pilots. The practice had been going on since flying started, and will continue long after I have gone and robots replace young men as commanders of airborne military equipment.

Any *stasieslet* worth his salt would know important things like this.

4
Becoming a chopper pilot

Before too long I was posted to South African Air Force College (SAAFCol) in Voortrekkerhoogte, Pretoria, alongside about 70 other newly qualified pilots and navigators for the prescribed SAAF Officer's Course.

At this stage, none of us had been commissioned and we still all wore the white shoulder tabs designating candidate officer, the rank we'd all held since starting the Pupe's Course. A week or two into the Officer's Course, a small Wings Parade was held and Brian King and I received our coveted SAAF Pilot's Wings.

The three-month Officer's Course was designed to smooth off the remaining rough edges that some of us still carried from the wide diversity of our upbringing and schooling, to teach us a few of the protocols necessary to be good junior officers, to equip us with some basic administrative skills, to get rid of some of the belly fat accumulated during the latter stages of the Pupe's Course, and, most importantly, to help us to survive formal dinners.

Attending lectures, completing syndicated projects and square-bashing on the parade ground, in roughly equal proportions, filled our days, while the nights were mostly spent acquainting ourselves with Pretoria's not inconsiderable pub and club life. Many happy hours were spent in such venerable hostelries as the Keg and Tankard, Rose and Crown, Crazy Horse Saloon, Bumpers, Grand Wazoo, Petticoat Lane, Zillertal, Jacqueline's and plenty of others whose names now escape me.

A nonsensical trend began to emerge whenever our group of 70-odd COs left the confines of the College on route marches that became longer and longer as we prepared for the 110-kilometre, five-day course-ending hike along and across the Magaliesberg, northwest of Pretoria. I use the word 'nonsensical' because of the insistence on the part of our drill instructors to do the training route marches at double pace for hours and hours on end.

It made no sense to any of my fellow pilots and navigators to trudge across hill and dale at a brutal rate for an extended period of time when our enormously expensive training – and future deployment – dictated that we move from place to place by air, even in the slowest aircraft, covering these distances in seconds or, at most, maybe just a few minutes. It was a question of energy efficiency, and the drill instructors just didn't seem to grasp the concept.

Brigadier Tony Roux pins my pilot wings to my chest.

After all the intensity, expectation and excitement of the Pupe's Course, there was no way on earth that the Officer's Course was going to be anything but an anticlimactic, frustrating, progress-halting, three-month interlude for a group of young people eager to use their newly acquired flying skills in an operational setting at an SAAF squadron.

A devil-may-care attitude came to prevail among most of the aircrew delegates. After all, we reasoned, if it is now discovered that you are not officer material, what are the higher-ups going to do? Fire you? Make you an NCO? Not a chance, after all the effort and money invested in training competent pilots and navigators. So, few of us bothered to stretch ourselves very much.

The one thing of value learnt at SAAFCol, and which we spent a lot of our time working out, was how to short-cut the system (for example, how to acquire and share exam questionnaires and answers before the exams were written) and not get caught. In the event of being caught out for some indiscretion or other, we practised long and hard to display, automatically and unthinkingly, the blank 'I-don't-understand-I'm-just-a-dumb-CO' facial expression and body posture. (This skill also came in handy when I was commissioned as a second lieutenant.)

The day I got my wings. *From the left*: my gran, Una Joubert; my dad, Pierre; me; my mom, Inez; my sister, Debbie and my brother, Mark.

And then, just before the relative inactivity really became unbearable, SAAFCol was in the past and we were all (unsurprisingly) qualified to become commissioned officers. However, one final, and key, component remained to be announced before we left for the next phase of our flying careers. What aircraft category would we be flying operationally?

There were four main options: jet aircraft, light aircraft, transport aircraft and helicopters. Selection to the individual categories was based on a combination of factors, including the psychological profile of the pilot, stated preference of the pilot, recommendations of the Pupe's Course instructor, the pilot's Pupe's Course ranking and squadron vacancies

Somehow, a combination of factors determined that I would fly helicopters, and so I was posted to 87 Advanced Flying School (AFS) at AFB Bloemspruit, outside Bloemfontein, to learn to fly this awesome category of flying machine. My instructor was Captain Kukes Dreyer, a vastly experienced and widely respected chopper pilot.

Having successfully completed the initial two-week 87 AFS ground school preparation, the day dawned for my first training flight on the single-turbine Aérospatiale Alouette III seven-seater chopper. Captain Dreyer, a flight engineer and I, flew out to a flat piece of ground to the east of AFB Bloemspruit.

Captain Dreyer brought the chopper into a stationary hover about two metres off the ground in the dead centre of the vast field.

'When I say, "You've got it", I want you to just take control and keep the chopper in exactly the same place until I give another instruction,' he said.

I remember thinking that this was a complete waste of time as I already had almost 400 hours of flying time. Asking me to keep an aircraft in one place was grossly underestimating my considerable (self-appraised) skills and was, in fact, insulting to my prowess as a qualified SAAF aviator.

'You've got it,' he said quietly.

The Aerospatiale Alouette III

I hadn't even managed to say, 'I've got it', when the Alo shot off sideways at a rate of knots. I immediately corrected and it screamed off in the opposite direction, climbing rapidly away from the ground as I fought for control.

I tried to arrest the climb and the Alo dived straight towards the ground.

'I've got it!' Captain Dreyer said, his voice slightly raised, immediately taking control of the aircraft and preventing imminent impact.

Over the next hour he showed me only one thing, and that was how to keep the chopper, more or less, in one place. It proved to be a difficult aircraft to get used to, and the controls were super-sensitive. The best practical advice Captain Dreyer gave me was 'Just think about the direction you want to go in and the Alo will go in that direction. You don't really have to consciously move the controls.'

So sensitive were the controls of the Alouette III that an experienced pilot could form a ring with their left-hand thumb and index finger around the shaft of the cyclic stick (joystick) and, without making contact with either thumb or forefinger, carry out all of the normal flying functions of the aircraft, including getting it into the air, progressing to full cruising speed, turning, slowing down and hovering just off the ground before completing the landing.

I was smitten from day one, and I relished every hour that I spent learning to fly this amazing aircraft.

Originally designed as an Alpine rescue helicopter, the Alo III had been reconfigured by the Rhodesian and South African armed forces to do a wide variety of jobs, ranging from maritime and mountain rescue to light transport to medevac to gunship. Of the roughly 2 000 logged hours that I have flown, either as pilot-in-command or as a co-pilot, without doubt the finest were while flying the Alo III, particularly in the Drakensberg on the border between South Africa and Lesotho.

But more about that later.

Learning to fly the Alo III was not easy. Even the most experienced of pilots battled to achieve more than a 70 per cent result in 'academic' flying tests. Academic flying is when you fly an aircraft in a strictly predetermined pattern of set speeds, headings, steepness of turns, rates of climb and descent, and precision landings. The sensitivity of the Alo's controls meant that just thinking, or not thinking – as the case may be – even for a split second, would cause the aircraft to deviate from the desired path. This made accurate academic flying nearly impossible to maintain for the duration of an academic flying test. Nevertheless, there was no compromising on the strict standards of the SAAF, and only those pilots who met these standards were permitted to fly any of the range of SAAF helicopters operationally. I am still proud to count myself among those few who believe that 'To fly is heavenly but to hover is … divine'.

To demonstrate the capabilities of the aircraft, Captain Dreyer once took me to a 'confined area landing zone' situated in a grove of eucalyptus trees close to the wall of Mocke's Dam, a small reservoir located about 30 kilometres east of Bloemfontein. Surveying the 'hole' in the middle of the 30-metre-high bluegums from the air, it seemed absolutely impossible to insert a hovering Alo into the available space, but Captain Dreyer seemed unperturbed. After determining the direction of the wind, we crept towards the opening, came to a stop immediately above it and then inched slowly downward. From this point on, most of the time my eyes were closed as I listened for the crunching sound of rotor blades striking tree trunk and anticipated the helpless dread of the death plunge that would follow as, bereft of lift, we hurtled earthwards to our demise.

But the next moment there was a slight bump and we landed, gently and quite safely, on a concrete base at the foot of the trees that normally served as a hardstand for tents at the Mocke's Dam camping site.

'When you know what you're doing in the Alo, you can come back and do this "confined" on your own,' Captain Dreyer advised.

Ja … right.

Flying in the mountains really tests an Alo III pilot's skills.

After the initial shock of its control sensitivity and quirky characteristics, I seemed to adapt quite well to the Alo III and really began relishing it as a mode of transport, even when, as an essential part of our training programme, our instructors started to randomly reduce engine power, at inopportune and inconvenient times, by pulling the engine fuel flow lever back to idle, simulating an engine failure. Your 'friends' in this situation are speed and height. The more of each that you have, the more safely, theoretically, a competent pilot can land the aircraft, by giving himself and the aircraft time to set up a life- and aircraft-saving autorotation.

The autorotation works similarly to the toy windmills that some of us had as kids. When you ran with them held out into the airflow, or pointed them into a wind or held them out of the window of a moving car, it spun a basic propeller or rotor on a spindle.

In the case of a helicopter, like the Alouette III, this kinetic-energy-induced rotation of the rotor, above a certain rpm and in the hands of a well-trained pilot, potentially creates sufficient lift to cushion the aircraft's impact with the ground in the event of engine failure. This is a finely balanced manoeuvre, and must be practised, in all phases of flight, frequently and repeatedly, in order for the pilot to build the confidence necessary to carry out the procedure correctly.

Mostly, these simulations of engine failure, for me at least, were life-lengthening. My heart always stopped dead with the hideous sound of the Alo's Artouste turbine engine suddenly spooling down and didn't get going again until we were safely on the ground in one piece. I reckon that if my heart didn't work at all during the many, many, many times that I practised auto-rotations, the combined effect would be that it would not wear out as quickly as that of pilots who were able to do auto-rotations without panicking.

Fortunately for me and the crews and passengers who flew

with me in the Alo over the next few years, none of us were ever required to depend on my skills as an 'autorotator' in the normal course of events. Again, I thank my guardian angel for that not inconsiderable mercy.

*

In the heady days of the late 1970s, the undoubted highlight of the 87 AFS Helicopter Course took place towards the end of the course, when, for two weeks, the entire school moved to Kelvin Grove, a country lodge just outside the town of Bergville, near the foot of the Drakensberg, owned by an ex-SAAF pilot named James Sclanders.

Rising up from the Natal midlands to a height of nearly 3 500 metres, the Drakensberg produces extremes of weather and changing flying conditions. For aspiring SAAF chopper pilots, the region represents the ultimate challenge to newly acquired flying skills. One moment you could be barrelling along in clear air, climbing progressively higher towards the Lesotho plateau, which lies atop the Drakensberg Escarpment, and the next you could be sucked into a 6 000 feet-per-minute (1 830 metres per minute) downdraft, which, if you did not immediately take emergency action, could cause your aircraft to slam into a rock face within seconds. One moment the sky could be a bright blue and the next you'd go around a mountain and the other side could be engulfed in a thick mist, blotting out visibility and leading almost certainly to the demise of the aircraft and crew. And all of this occurred in an environment of indescribable beauty and grandeur on an unmatched scale.

The ancient basalt formations such as Cathkin, Sterkhorn, Cathedral and the Eastern Buttress are visible from hundreds of kilometres away on a clear day, and hidden behind them are titanic gems such as Champagne Castle, Monk's Cowl, the Devil's Tooth and the Bell. Gatberg, situated at about 2 400 metres above sea level and along a precipitous ridge called the Dragon's Back, is a favourite photographic opportunity for helicopter crews, and landing atop its tiny platform is a feather in the cap for any chopper guy, novice or veteran.

Captain Dreyer had his own favourite spot. One day, while teaching me the rudiments of power loss at higher altitudes, he told me to relax, took the controls and headed full tilt for what appeared to be a sheer cliff face rising up between the massive Cathkin Peak and Champagne Castle and which I recognised as Monk's Cowl.

Reducing speed as we approached the Monk's Cowl rock face, which rises 1 200 metres from the saddle between the afore-mentioned peaks, the Alo crept forward and then entered a narrow chasm in the mountain, the sides of which were thousands of feet high and which had not been visible to us just seconds before. The floor of the chasm rose in seemingly endless steps above us and we slowly climbed into the half-light provided by a thin sliver of sky far above.

It was late June and the South African winter was well under way. In the upper reaches of the Berg this meant below-freezing temperatures throughout the day. As we flew ever higher up the hidden cleft, the water that coursed downwards in summer stood starkly solidified as ice, defying gravity, as if waiting for someone to flick a switch and release it into the valleys far below. Just when it seemed that it was about to become too dark to continue the climb, we came around a corner and the chasm opened out into a 200-metre-wide waterfall tumbling off the Lesotho plateau.

The entire extent of the waterfall had frozen into an intense azure hue off which the sunshine bounced like thousands of fairies dancing and twirling in an enormous and magical ballroom. Countless icicles, some as long as telephone poles, clung to the surrounding rocks, and the sudden brightness of the light stung our eyes and forced us to squint.

I realised that I was no longer breathing.

Captain Dreyer's landing on a small platform at the foot of the waterfall was the gentlest that I ever enjoyed. As the Alo's engine quietened and then stopped, none of us spoke at all, completely mesmerised, perhaps even hypnotised, by what was around us. How long we remained there in that trancelike state, or how long it stayed with us, I can't remember. But the experience is encapsulated in a line from Shakespeare's *The Tempest*, in which Caliban says, 'And when I woke, I cried to dream again.' The Monk's Cowl experience that June afternoon was a priceless gift and the indisputable highlight of my SAAF flying career.

Back at Kelvin Grove things tended to get hectic. Often.

87 AFS had brought along an entire team of chefs, as well as bar and kitchen staff, to cater to our every food and drink need. When the flying duties for the day were over, students, instructors and guests gathered in the pub. Sedgewick's Old Brown Sherry was a particular favourite, and was consumed faster than it could be delivered.

Major Sclanders had a pesky, semi-domesticated pied crow, which had an irritating habit of picking up our packets of newly opened cigarettes, typically Camel Filter, in its beak. It would then fly up to the apex of the nearest roof or onto a rafter, where it would proceed to extract the smokes one at a time, taking care to break each cigarette neatly in the middle, before discarding the pieces.

No amount of shouting or throwing beer cans and stones deterred the crow, and stronger countermeasures were contemplated as a matter of necessity and urgency. Nothing seemed to be effective during our first week at Kelvin Grove, and it took until after Sunday lunch, and quite a few drinks, for Captain Dreyer to come up with a solution.

Somewhere he had managed to unearth an R1 semi-automatic assault rifle and a box of 7.62 mm plastic rounds, which he loaded into the 20-round magazine and then set off in pursuit of 'that feathered fucker'. A one-sided firefight ensued, but every round that Captain Dreyer fired missed the crow, which, totally unperturbed, continued merrily on its path of wanton destruction. A fellow student named Robin 'Flop' Laatz, strolled along behind Captain Dreyer, beer in hand, offering a running combination of witty advice and personal insult each time a shot went wide of the mark.

Finally, an exasperated Captain Dreyer, possibly suffering from sense-of-humour failure, rounded on Flop, who was standing about 25 metres away.

'You couldn't hit a cow in the c**t with a banjo!' trumpeted Flop. Then, raising his can of beer away from his body, at just above head height and to the side, he taunted Captain Dreyer: 'Shoot this, William Tell!'

A shot rang out and a bullet hole appeared dead-centre in the middle of the beer can. Simultaneously, an incredulous expression came over Flop's face as he looked down at his hand.

'You shot me, you *doos!*' Flop mumbled, before slowly sinking to the ground and staring fixedly at the bloodied stump where the tip of his left thumb had been.

Chopper crews are a notoriously tight lot and will always draw an impenetrable defensive circle whenever they, or any of their number, are threatened. The incident involving Flop's loss of his thumb-tip was evidence of that bond.

Flop was taken to Ladysmith Hospital for treatment by the only relatively sober aircrew available and returned later that evening, bloodied but unbowed. The official investigation into the circumstances produced a frustrating maze of inconclusive findings. Vague, contradictory and highly varied recollections of the facts were provided by eyewitnesses, none of whom it seems had even heard a shot or seen a rifle. Captain Dreyer was a little more careful with a firearm after that, and many years would pass before anyone who was there would disclose what had actually happened.

Suitably equipped with a whole new set of skills related to operating an Alo III at higher-than-normal altitude, we ended our

12-day sojourn at Kelvin Grove. All the crews flew on to Durban for the weekend where more fun was had in places such as the Father's Moustache, the Beach Hotel and the Pool Bar at the Lonsdale Hotel.

*

We returned to Bloemfontein the following Monday and dived straight into the preparation for the final phase of the Chopper Course, which was to finish with a two-and-a-half-hour final test specifically designed to expose any shortcomings in the fledgling pilot's arsenal.

Navigation was one of the more challenging aspects of the test.

Unlike most aircraft, helicopters flying in an operational setting seldom climb to a height of more than 215 feet (65 metres) above the ground. Mostly, the Alouette III was flown at about half that height, necessitating a high degree of spatial and locational awareness on the part of the crew. Flying this low also severely limited your field of vision and made navigation, without any of the aids modern pilots have become accustomed to, an extremely difficult task. The Alo III had a magnetic compass and a gyroscopic direction indicator. Together with the air speed indicator, these formed the full range of electronic navigational aids available to us pilots. That was it. No navigation technologies such as VOR (Very high frequency Omni-directional Radio beacon), GPS (Global Positioning System) or INS (Inertial Navigation System) and nothing but heading and time – 'dead-reckoning' old-style navigation at its original and frantic best.

Preflight preparation for navigating along a particular route involved first marking turning points on a plastic-laminated 1:50 000 map with a chinagraph pencil (wax crayon). Then you would draw straight lines between the successive points with a long plastic ruler (or anything with a straight edge), marking off the progressive distance in nautical-mile increments (one nautical mile equals approximately 1.95 kilometres), noting also the corresponding time-to-fly calculations and measuring the magnetic heading for each leg using a plastic protractor. The map would be folded in such a way as to allow the pilot to 'page over' when reaching the end of a map segment and expose the next section of the desired route. At a cruising speed of 85 knots (roughly 160 kph), not fast in anyone's imagination, it was still all too easy to lose track and end up at the wrong place at the wrong time, something I was reasonably adept at doing.

In my final test on the Alo III Chopper Course, the examination was conducted by a legendary testing officer and instructor called Major Piet Klaasen, known far and wide for his magnificent moustache and rich Malmesbury *bry* (burr, pronounced 'bray'). Unbeknown to the good major, I had been detained, for reasons I will conveniently overlook, in the nurses' residence of a teaching hospital in Bloemfontein during the previous night. I had escaped by shimmying down a drain pipe from a fourth-floor room just in time to make it back to AFB Bloemspruit, shower and run up to the flight line to await the imminent arrival of the testing officer.

I did not have long to wait. The flight engineer who was to accompany us advised me to direct my breathing away from the testing officer when he arrived lest he detect the pungent evidence of my previous evening's quite obvious overindulgence.

Major Klaasen arrived and the test commenced. We started off with a three-leg navigation exercise to the northeast of Bloemfontein. The temperature was hovering around the 7°C mark, there was no blue sky at all, and the cloud base was at only about 90 metres. Thick mist obscured the tops of even the smallest hills, and there was a strong westerly wind blowing. The combined effects of the meteorological conditions, sleep deprivation and a raging hangover were to expose my limited navigation prowess even more than would have been the case in sunny weather. As the wind was coming hard from the port side, at almost right angles to the desired track, I countered this by positioning the nose of the Alo a little into the wind in the vain hope that I had 'guesstimated' the offset angle correctly and the aircraft would accurately (magically?) follow the chosen path to the first turning point, located about 40 nautical miles (74 kilometres) away.

So, I initiated a slight turn to the left.

I tried to match the natural features, such as hills and rivers, that we were passing on the ground with the corresponding symbols and squiggles on the map unfolding on my knee, but it all rapidly became a blurred jumble of confusion.

So, I turned a little further left.

Halfway through the leg I thought (erroneously) that I recognised a hill-and-stream combination that seemed to correspond to the map. It showed that I was right of the track.

So, I turned a little more to the left.

Major Klaasen said nothing. He just sat there, as was his role, and observed me turn left. Then left again, and then left again.

Finally, we emerged from a gap between two cloud-covered hills and a small town appeared directly in front of us. My navigation skills were such that I knew there were no towns anywhere close to the track that the aircraft was supposed to be on.

'I think that I have drifted off track,' I mumbled into the microphone.

The group who did the helicopter course at 87 Advanced Flying School with me (I'm at the back, fourth from the left).

'No shit, Sherrrrrrrrrrlock!' guffawed the major.

'Do you go to Prrrrrretorrrrrria on the weekends?' he asked.

'Yes. Sometimes.' I replied.

'Then you should rrrrrrrrrecognise the town of Brrrrrrrrrrrandfort! We are now only 18 miles off trrrrrrrack! That is a worrrrrrrrld rrrrrrrrecord deviation for a 40-mile leg! Congrrrrrrrrratulations!' he trumpeted with great mirth and a total absence of malice.

Repositioning to where we were supposed to be, I managed to progress through the remaining two legs of the navigation exercise without further incident. Major Klaasen then put me through my paces in rigorously testing the full range of my newly accumulated Alo III flying skills, and declared that I had managed to meet the minimum standards demanded.

All that remained was for me to redo the navigation section of the test, albeit on a very different and more difficult route, which I did successfully the following day.

A popular social expression at the time was to ask someone who'd just demonstrated some cleverness, 'So, does that make you a chopper pilot?' I could now truthfully reply in the affirmative.

*

I really loved the Alo III, but, the next step towards an operational flying role in the SAAF was converting to the far larger and infinitely more sophisticated Aérospatiale Puma. The twin-engine, twin-pilot Puma was a state-of-the art medium-category military helicopter capable of fulfilling multiple operational roles, primarily in deploying up to 16 heavily armed soldiers onto the battlefield. It was flown by a breed of extraordinarily brave men.

Upon successful completion of a Puma conversion course at 19 Squadron B Flight at AFB Swartkop, the plan was that we newly qualified Puma pilots would be deployed to an operational SAAF squadron as co-pilots, also called *sandsakke* (sandbags or ballast) for approximately two years, after which – with sufficient experience and competence – we would be able to apply for a command (captaincy) of this fine aircraft.

My course mates all seemed to love this powerful aircraft and all its electronic and instrumental sophistication. However, from the outset of the conversion course, I dreaded the idea of sitting in the Puma's left-hand seat for the next two years. My enthusiasm continued to wane as the course progressed, fortunately not to the detriment of my ability to fly the Puma but sufficiently so for me to take a firm decision to take remedial action at the first available opportunity.

That moment arrived within minutes of my completing the final flying test on the course. I walked determinedly into the office of the squadron commander, the legendary Major 'Monster' Wilkens, and asked him to help me transfer to 17 Squadron, which was stationed just a short distance away.

'But they fly the Alo!' he said with some surprise.

'Their pilots log pilot-in-command hours, sir,' I replied. 'And they are all commanders.'

'Are you absolutely certain that you want to go to 17?' he asked.

'Yes, I am, sir.'

He looked at me for quite a long time and asked if I'd like to take a day or two to reconsider this unprecedented and drastic step.

'I want to fly Alos, sir, and thinking about it for a few days won't change that decision.'

'Well, okay then. I'll give the 17 Squadron OC (officer commanding) a call and see how amenable he is to your request and I'll get back to you.'

'Please call him now, Major?' I pleaded.

He looked at me quizzically, perhaps even with a shade of pity, then picked up the phone and called Commandant André Bekker, OC 17 Squadron. After a brief conversation, during which he outlined my insane request, he asked me, 'Commandant Bekker would like to know how many hours you have?'

'Almost 500, sir,' I responded quickly, knowing full well that the absolute minimum required to get an operational command on choppers in the SAAF was normally 500 hours. I actually had around 497 hours at the time, thanks to having accumulated an extra 150 or so hours in the few months I'd spent at CFS Dunnottar's Station Flight doing test flights with the *stasieslette* and grabbing every 'jolly-ride' in sight.

After he put the phone down, Major Wilkens looked at me and said, 'Commandant Bekker is happy to give you a chance, but you need to go there right now and then pass their 17 Squadron competency test today.'

By the time he got to 'competency test today' I was already out of the door and bound for the 17 Squadron buildings, situated just 300 metres away. I was immediately sent into the hangar to familiarise myself with the Alo III again. Once I'd gone over the aircraft operating protocols and emergency procedures a few times on my own in a stationary aircraft, the 17 Squadron instructor put me through an intensive and probing two-hour evaluation of my Alo III competency.

My luck held. I passed the assessment and was immediately welcomed to the squadron as a fully-fledged Alo III commander.

The downside was that, the very next day, I boarded a Safair Lockheed L-100-30 troop-carrying aircraft (the civilian version of the C-130), known as a 'Flossie', and flew 2 000 kilometres to Ondangwa in Ovamboland, the centre of airborne operations in far northern South West Africa (today Namibia) during the Border War, for the first of many operational tours.

For just over two decades, I had enjoyed the privilege of growing up in circumstances that sheltered me from the unsavoury realities faced by so many of my countrymen on a daily basis. I'd never been required to take the political situation in South Africa seriously at all.

That was about to change.

Part II
Time to grow up

5
Into the fray

Although I was not yet aware of it, at this early stage of my career there was already ample evidence of my discomfort with the military way of doing things. Consequently, I often ran up against the military's strict protocols, and faced censure for it. Perhaps I have my mom to thank for this, as she raised me to question everything that I didn't understand. The result was that I was never able to swallow the military's ideological story. My personal political principles, as poorly developed as they were, rebelled against the prevailing conservatism. Although I had learnt to keep my beliefs strictly to myself, I found it difficult to hide my contemptuous expression when confronted with orders and opinions that I disrespected.

This is not to say that I was a raging liberal masquerading as a military officer. I just felt that there was more to life than the military and that I, rather than they, should determine the path I followed. I had read Ayn Rand's novel *The Fountainhead* for the first time in my mid-teens, and had come to the conclusion that, like the novel's protagonist, Howard Roark, I was an avid objectivist. To me, this meant that you cannot control much of what happens to you in life but that you are totally responsible for how you respond to life's challenges. So, I would hoe my own furrow and accept the consequences of doing so.

But I was totally ignorant of how hard it would be to do so in the South African Air Force.

*

I arrived at AFB Ondangwa – my home for the next three months – for the first time just after lunch on an early November day in 1979. The temperature stood at a steaming-hot 38°C.

115

I was 21 years old.

The Flossie that had brought me there had approached AFB Ondangwa, still called 95 TAU (Tactical Airfield Unit) at the time, after a brief pit stop at AFB Grootfontein, 200 kilometres to the south, at an altitude of around 25 000 feet (7 620 metres). Once over Ondangwa, the Flossie pilots closed the throttles on the aircraft's four Allison turbine engines and flung the aircraft into a steep, left-hand spiral turn. In just two of these gut-wrenching circuits, at almost breakneck speed, they lined up the large aircraft on a short final approach to Runway 06 and smoothly 'greased' the wheels onto the 2.4-kilometre-long tarmac. Once the wheels were on the ground, the pilot slammed the propellers into reverse pitch and stood on the brakes to bring the shuddering white-and-orange Hercules down to a speed safe enough to turn off the runway and taxi to the enormous concrete hardstand situated just to the south of the main runway.

When the engines had all been shut down, the cavernous jaws of the cargo loading ramp at the rear of the aircraft opened and loadmasters began to discharge the on-board freight. A crew member opened the small door near the front of the aircraft on the left-hand side, from which most of the passengers aboard disembarked.

I exited into the brightest sunshine that I'd ever experienced. The first thing that struck me was not the rows of parked and armed combat aircraft and helicopters stretching off into the distance, but rather the cornea-incinerating glare from the white sand that covered every unpaved space. It was impossible to see without sunglasses, and I immediately understood the foresight of some Ondangwa predecessor in convincing the SAAF to issue high-quality Ray-Bans to all personnel.

Before I could follow the other passengers, who were making their way towards a large arrivals hall, I was approached by an Air Force major in a nutria-brown uniform.

'Baz Newham,' he introduced himself. 'I am the Ondangs CO. You must be Joubert. Please show me which bags belong to you.'

Startled, I followed him as he moved towards the cargo pallets that the loadmasters were unloading. A cursory search produced my only piece of luggage, a kitbag, which contained a few work and casual clothes and some basic toiletries.

'Is that all?' he asked, and I showed him my Nomex flying bag in which I had hand-carried my flying helmet, boots and gloves in the passenger cabin.

'I travel light, sir.'

'Good,' he said. 'Come with me,' and he set off towards the line of parked Alo III gunships that I could see about 400 metres away.

On the way there, he briefed me.

'I am told that you do not yet have the required 500 hours which you need for an ops command. How many do you have exactly?'

'Uhhhhh … 499 and a quarter, Major,' I said, somewhat tentatively.

'Then you will have to get into that Alo there,' he said, 'and stay airborne, within the confines of this airbase, for at least 45 minutes.'

One of the tasks of Alo gunship crews at Ondangwa was to ensure that aircraft landing and departing, like the Flossie, did so without being shot out of the sky by the guerrilla fighters of the People's Liberation Army of Namibia (PLAN), the military wing of the South West African People's Organisation (SWAPO). The guerrillas were mostly Ovambo tribesmen from Ovamboland, and moved quite freely among the local population, wreaking their own special brand of havoc from time to time. However, so effective a deterrent was the Alo III gunship 'top cover' counter at Ondangwa, and at other SAAF bases in the operational area, that no aircraft were ever attacked there.

So, without even changing into a flying overall, I did as Major Baz instructed. When I landed after the departure of the Flossie, 45 minutes later, I was deemed to be 'operationally legal' and instantly became the greenest greenhorn gunship pilot in the SAAF.

I will be eternally grateful to the gentle shepherding, preferential treatment and covert protection that Newham and others at AFB Ondangwa afforded me over the course of the next three months, as I assimilated a wealth of tricks and shortcuts from the older, more experienced pilots without being blown from the African sky.

There was no greater manifestation of this special care than the allocation to me, as my 'partner' flight engineer, of Flight Sergeant Flip Pretorius, a large, immensely strong and battle-proven warrior-among-men. I probably learnt more about life, about the technical stresses to which an Alo is exposed in bush war conditions, and about the tireless commitment to ensuring its ongoing serviceability from Flip, the other flight engineers and ground crew, in that first three months, than in the rest of my career combined.

So green was I with respect to the challenging local flying conditions, and so blissfully unaware of the fact, that I almost crashed the Alo III 'trooper' that I flew on my first mission out of Ondangwa. The 'trooper' was an Alo III configured for light passenger transport or 'walking wounded' casualty evacuation, and it had only a small .303 machine gun mounted in the left-hand sliding door for protection.

My mission, a day or two after my arrival at Ondangwa, required that I fly the Alo about 100 kilometres northeast to a small South African army base called Nkongo, just south of the Angolan border, where I was to collect a senior and very fierce army officer, Colonel 'Witkop' Badenhorst, and his aide. I was then to fly them 110 kilometres due westwards to Eenhana, another army base located just a few kilometres south of the border.

At around 11h00 I took off from Ondangs with the air temperature hovering around 40°C. When I got to Nkongo I performed a hover (vertical) landing onto a concrete slab inside the five-metre-high protective perimeter wall, called a revetment, which secluded the interior of the base from prying eyes outside.

There was a 25-metre-wide gap in the revetment that led to a 1 000-metre-long paved runway. At the time, I strongly believed that no self-respecting chopper pilot would ever use a runway, like a normal aircraft, unless it became absolutely necessary.

Now, Colonel Badenhorst was a large man. As was his aide. And so was Flip. It was also extremely hot and dry. The combined effect of all these factors, I should already have known, had I been listening carefully when the subject of density altitude was discussed on the Chopper Course, instead of dreamily contemplating hidden accesses to nurses' residences, was to rob the Nkongo air of most of its available lift.

My passengers boarded and I started up. Once I'd completed the pre-take-off checks I lifted the trooper off the ground and onto a cushion of air called 'ground effect', which helps to keep hovering helicopters airborne while stationary. However, as soon as I pushed the cyclic stick forward to initiate forward momentum, blissfully unaware of the impending disaster, the Alo simply 'fell off' the supporting cushion of air and refused to go anywhere, let alone accelerate smoothly and climb gracefully over the concrete and steel revetment.

I realised that something was terribly wrong, and at the last possible moment hoofed the right rudder pedal as hard as I could to prevent the Alo's imminent impact with the wall. The aircraft immediately spun around to point the way it had just come, miraculously missing various pieces of structure, each of which could have caused serious damage or even injury and loss of life.

The deathly silence that followed the near accident was finally broken by Flip suggesting quietly, 'Loot, let's just pretend that we're a fixed-wing and go take off on the runway like the big boys do?'

Just days after the Nkongo incident, I crossed into Angola for the first of what would be countless visits over the coming years. It was standard practice that junior pilots like me would fly as 'wingmen' to more experienced pilots and learn the ropes from the *oumanne* (older guys). This practice, dating back to the early days of combat aviation, placed the onus for protecting the leader's backside on his wingman. During the Border War, we strictly applied this principle and never crossed into enemy territory alone. There was always another aircraft to partner with you.

On this particular mission, both the formation leader and I were flying Alo III gunships, which each spouted 20 mm Oerlikon or Hispano side-firing cannons in the gap where the left-hand sliding door would normally be. We also carried around 250 rounds of ammunition in a 'pan' located on the floor in the front left of the helicopter.

We departed from the airfield at Ruacana, crossed the border just east of the Calueque Dam wall and continued for 70 kilometres northwards. We were flying at low level just to the east of the Kunene River (Portuguese spelling: Cunene) to a rendezvous point where we were to climb up to the Alo III's most effective 'fighting' height of 600–800 feet (200–250 metres) above ground level (AGL) and give cover to a formation of Pumas that would be landing a company of our troops there. 'Cover' normally meant that the gunships arrived ten to fifteen minutes before the Pumas and we did our level best to ensure that there were no enemy anti-aircraft weapons or hostile troops awaiting their arrival.

The map of the area that we had that day was rudimentary at best and was held by the gunship formation leader, Lieutenant 'Boats' Olivier. It was a photocopy of a 30-year-old depiction of the area, hand-drawn by a Portuguese colonial land surveyor. Nevertheless, how hard could it be to find the designated landing zone (LZ) on terrain as flat as a pancake, where two well-used dirt roads intersected at right angles about 65 kilometres into Angola? The compass heading that we were following was only marginally important, as by keeping the north–south road below us and the huge expanse of the Kunene River just 200 metres to the west positioned us almost exactly above the desired track.

The far more important issue should have been the time required to fly to the target, but even that was largely disregarded as the map's scale of distance seemed dubious and inaccurate. So, we relied heavily on the one clearly evident thing we had – the impossible-to-miss crossroads of the north–south and east–west roads right on the landing zone.

It was only in the aftermath of this event that we were to discover that the east–west road had fallen into disuse at least 20 years before and had become overgrown with riverine bush, completely obscuring it from aerial detection. We flashed by the LZ completely oblivious to that fact.

Another aspect that had escaped our pre-mission preparation was the looming presence of FAPLA (People's Armed Forces for the Liberation of Angola) troops in the fortified town of Vila Roçadas (later Xangongo), situated just ten kilometres north of our intended LZ. From the missed LZ to the town at the cruising speed of the Alo III would take less than four minutes.

We ploughed nonchalantly onwards.

That day, my guardian angel decided to put in a most timeous and fortuitous appearance. We had just commenced the climb to 'gun height' (approximately 200 metres) and I was patiently waiting for Boats to begin the orbit around the LZ when suddenly it felt like I had been punched in the stomach. In that moment, I heard a woman's voice inside my head screaming, 'Get away! Get out of here!'

'Boats, we've got to turn around,' I yelled on the radio.

'We're not there yet,' Boats responded.

'We're at the LZ and there is no sign of you guys!' interrupted the concerned Puma formation leader. Then he barked out, 'Wherever you are, get down and away from there. Immediately!'

Without a second's hesitation both Boats and I turned sharply towards the south and dived for terra firma. Seconds later, the clear blue sky into which we had been heading erupted in a hellish scene of smoke, flame, exploding rocket-propelled grenades (RPGs) and tracer bullets. Had we continued on that path our aircraft would almost certainly have been blasted from the southern Angolan sky.

The split-second decision to escape gave us the time we needed to dive steeply for the trees and set a heading due southwards for the relative safety of the border, as fast as our little Alos could carry us. I know that it is not possible to fly below ground level in any aircraft, but in the 30 minutes that followed, Boats and I did the next best thing – dodging between the low acacia trees and scrubby little bushes pockmarking the arid landscape, all the way back across the border and to the airfield at Ruacana. There we quickly refuelled and set course for our primary base at Ondangwa.

I remember at the time not being aware, or even conscious, of the sequence of events that had transpired over the previous hour or two. My brain seemed numb, as if a local anaesthetic had somehow been applied to everything around me. I felt like I was watching myself from a distance of a few metres away, going through the motions of flying the chopper as a robot might.

We completed the flight back to Ondangwa without further incident and landed just before sundown. I headed immediately for the pub, ate a tasteless supper and consumed an unprecedented quantity of gin and tonic, without its having any effect on me whatsoever. Much later, in the witching hours of that night, I lay awake, wide-eyed in the cocooned refuge that was my mosquito-net-enclosed, cold-steel, military-issue bed in the darkened, prefabricated 'terrapin' billet at Ondangwa. There, I was finally invisible to the sharp eyes of my more experienced colleagues, who might otherwise have spotted all the newfound doubt and fear that had suddenly become my unwelcome companion. I felt suddenly stripped bare of my self-belief. Only then did the mechanism in my brain that controls these things begin to review, in graphic detail, frame by frame, the full sequence of our most fortunate escape.

As the full-colour scenes rolled by across the movie screen of my visual cortex, the tendrils of fear of what might have been and the resultant tremors of shock from the attack, for which I had obviously been neither accustomed to nor in the least prepared for, threatened to overwhelm me and reduce me to a shivering, whimpering and terrified little child. I bit down hard and gritted my teeth to stop them chattering and squeezed my eyes closed so tightly that my temples hurt, hoping that the nightmare images would magically just disappear. But they kept on playing, for how long I really don't know. I wanted so badly for them to stop.

Then, suddenly, just when it seemed certain that I would start to blubber uncontrollably and cry out aloud into the Ovamboland night, a wondrous thing happened. Like a light being extinguished, the horror movie and all the anguish just stopped. One moment I was panicking and in a world of anguish and the next I felt the panic subside and the blessed relief of all emotion draining from me, leaving me feeling nothing ... absolutely nothing at all.

I found out years later, from a psychologist friend particularly skilled in this area of human behaviour, that it was my 'sensory overload switch' activating for the first time. It would do so countless times in the years that followed. When the switch was activated, all the conflicting and frightening emotions that I was feeling were immediately cut off. This proved to be a priceless blessing in the circumstances prevailing at the time – and for the next few years.

*

Lurking at the periphery of all I did, learnt and experienced during my military years was a paranoid terror of accidentally violating the Official Secrets Act, to which all SADF soldiers were subject. Such was my fear that I would not even participate in any informal discussions with colleagues on subjects like politics, the war itself and its likely outcome, anything to do with apartheid, the influence of the church or questions related to the strategies and objectives followed by our military leaders. Not that these kinds of discussions were commonplace. On the contrary, I think most of us involved, at least at junior officer level, felt enormously discouraged from questioning the status quo.

Consequently, little photographic evidence of any phase of activity in the operational area was recorded, and media reports on events that took place were rare. Access to day-to-day developments in the Border War was limited to a few authorised personnel. Those of us who participated in the fighting were under threat of severe prison terms, or worse, should it come to light that we had discussed our experiences with anyone – friend, family or even professional counsellor.

So, as far as family, friends and even the majority of young men who spent time in the operational area south of the Yati Strip, also known as 'the cutline' (the 100-metre-wide, 440-kilometre-long zone that formed the border between South West Africa and Angola between Ruacana and Katwitwi in the Caprivi Strip), were concerned, we spent our days drinking copious quantities of cheap booze (five cents a tot for Beefeater gin, for example), puffing away at Camel Filters (20 cents for a packet of 20) and acquiring a deep bronze tan, using a mixture of brake fluid and used cooking oil as suntan lotion. We also busied ourselves with finding innovative ways of disposing of the compulsory stocks of anti-malarial Daramal, because we believed that Daramal caused our hard-earned tans to fade too soon.

I also learnt to curse for 60 seconds straight without repeating a single swearword, fantasised endlessly about what I'd do with it if I ever got hold of whatever was hidden behind the strategically placed black stars in *Scope* magazine, and, like most of the other chaps there, remained firmly seated on the ground for a long time after watching the odd blue movie smuggled into the base by our own resident Radar O'Reilly (a character in *M*A*S*H*).

Days turned into weeks and the weeks into months, and the daily routine of an Alo pilot based in Ondangwa didn't vary much. Normally, I was awake by 05h00. After showering, shaving and brushing my teeth, I'd go down to the operations briefing room with the other crews, where I'd wolf down a cup or two of steaming tea or coffee (sometimes it was difficult to tell the difference), accompanied by biscuits and rusks and small dried-out sandwiches. There we'd all receive the day's flying activity

The only photo of me (that I know of) with the Alouette III.

briefing. Then it was to the aircraft for the pre-flight check and back to the technical hut to sign the F700 form, by virtue of which you accepted that the aircraft allocated to you was serviceable and flight-ready. Take-off followed as soon as all formation participants were ready to go.

It was rare to have a day off, and even when this luxury was bestowed you would almost certainly still be required for stand-by duties. If you did have a day off, your primary concern was to sleep in as late as practically possible, ease into the day when it got too hot to remain submerged under the mosquito net, and later repair gently towards the small splash pool located adjacent to the accommodations. 'Nothing rushed' was the strict order on those days.

So, when news reached us that AFB Ondangwa had a new RSM it barely raised a blip on the chopper pilots' radar. This news was particularly overshadowed when the operations officer informed all Alo crews that there would be no flying for us the next day. In our minds, the two events were not even remotely linked.

The advisory to the chopper pilots, delivered just before closing time in the pub, that the new RSM intended holding an inspection parade at the officers' terrapin quarters the following morning, on a rest day, was dismissed with the contempt it rightly deserved. At precisely 07h00, while we were all still deeply asleep, the new RSM marched smartly up to the door of our digs, crashed to a thunderous halt, ripped the door open and shouted, as only an RSM could, at decibel levels bordering on the criminally negligent:

'OFFICERS ... ATTEN ... SHUN!'

A few seconds of dead silence followed and so he shouted again, even louder than before, 'OFFICERS ... ATTEN ... SHUN!!!!!'

'Fuck off!' said the eight-strong pilot complement of the two adjoining terrapins simultaneously.

'I am the RSM and I am authorised to inspect the officers' quarters with adequate warning!' wailed the startled but still indignant man. 'And I gave the notification to you all in the pub last night!'

'If you come through that door, we will fucking shoot you!' someone shouted.

Discretion being the better part of valour, the RSM immediately stalked off in a great huff to Major Newham, who later told us what had transpired.

'Major, the chopper pilots are undermining my attempts to improve discipline!' the RSM whined when he entered Newham's office.

'What happened?' Major Baz asked quietly.

The RSM puffed up his ample chest, stood smartly to attention, staring straight ahead, and related the exact details of the events of the preceding minutes.

Then Major Newham, in measured tones, said, 'RSM, if you ever again tell my chopper drivers to ready themselves for an inspection by you or anyone else, without discussing it with me, and particularly on one of their off days, I will shoot you myself!'

*

The main road that connected South West Africa to Angola ran north from Windhoek through the town of Ondangwa, and then skirted the Ondangs airfield just to the east of it, before heading almost dead straight northwards to the border at Oshikango Gate. The border post on the Angolan side is still called Santa Clara, and five or so kilometres into Angola is the small town of Namacunde.

Intelligence sources had reported that a large group of PLAN soldiers was gathering just across the border. A raid was planned by the SADF to deal with the proximity threat they posed and to discourage the meeting. As raids go, this was a small one, and only two chopper gunships were allocated to provide air support to about 200 infantrymen, supported by a few Buffel landmine-protected troop carriers and a handful of Eland armoured cars.

The Eland, a South African-built, modernised version of a French design, was colloquially known to the troops as the 'Noddy car'.

It was my first operation.

The mission briefing took place at a brand-new army base called New Etale. The old Etale base, located nearby, was due to be closed and all troops stationed there moved to the New Etale base, which was better positioned and resourced. During the briefing, I didn't really know what to expect. I was the nominated wingman to Captain Chris Stroebel, an experienced chopper formation leader.

'Stay at 600–800 feet AGL and take up a position 180 degrees opposite me in the orbit around the target,' advised Chris. 'Look for anything threatening or out of the ordinary and make certain that it's the enemy you're looking at before you open fire. If you're unsure, rather don't shoot because there's no way to undo a 20 mm's mistake,' he added.

I remembered this sound counsel, and offered it to other newbies throughout my gunship career.

The raid was launched at around 11h00 with the Buffel-mounted infantrymen rushing across the cutline from two crossing points situated about 1 500 metres apart. Once in the vicinity of the PLAN gathering, their brief was to debus rapidly, spread out and encircle the PLAN fighters and cut off the escape route of the enemy soldiers caught in the pincer movement.

The role of the Noddy cars was to drive right into the middle of the conflict and cause havoc.

As gunships, our job was to provide air support to the troops on the ground and to give an overall view of the unfolding fight to the battle commander sitting on the ammunition box in Chris's chopper.

As the Noddy cars approached the border, I remembered that one of the instructions issued to vehicle commanders at the earlier briefing was for all combat vehicles to avoid driving on the road crossing the border at any cost. So, when I noticed a Noddy car driving up the tarred road through the no-man's land between the two opposing border posts, being a rookie and without a shred of battlefield experience, I contemplated calling out a warning on the radio to the vehicle crew, but didn't, for fear that I might make a fool of myself.

Seconds later, the Noddy car reached the boom across the road at the Angolan border post and detonated the multiple landmines buried beneath it. The Noddy car flew straight up into the air, borne aloft by a boiling, roiling cloud of black and orange smoke and flame, slowly twisting around like it wanted to look at the gaping hole that had suddenly appeared on the spot where it had just been. It seemed to hesitate for a few seconds at the apex before it crashed down onto its roof in a shower of sparks, instantly killing two of its three occupants.

In a countryside as flat as Ovamboland, the tell-tale signature of a landmine detonation, a dark-grey spearhead rising vertically above the incident site, is visible from up to 70 kilometres away and can be seen within seconds of the detonation occurring. It is my most unfortunate reality to have observed a number of these abominations and to have arrived on the scene within minutes of the blast. In my opinion, the burying of landmines and improvised explosive devices (IEDs) on public roads is one of the most depraved and immoral features of warfare.

My second encounter with the landmine scourge happened just a few weeks into my first operational tour and occurred on Oom Willie se pad between Eenhana and Oshikango. A vehicle laden with local Ovambo residents – men, women and children returning from a shopping trip to a nearby market – had detonated a landmine. There were no survivors, and no amount of effort by the medical rescue teams could determine the number of casualties, their genders or their ages. It was not even possible to identify the make of vehicle, although we were later informed it was a Toyota light delivery vehicle. Wreckage from the vehicle, body parts and the tattered remains of the occupants' purchases were strewn over a radius of 300 metres from the blast site.

The impression still retained in my memory bank today, nearly 40 years later, is of a distorted and indescribably violent nightmare scene where everything – trees, bushes, metal and flesh – had been shredded, as if a giant food processor had brought its spinning blades to bear on this small patch of African soil.

The scale of destruction that I witnessed that day shattered forever any illusions I may have had about the morality of conflict between people, no matter how complicated the issues involved might be. Surely we humans are better than this?

But the switch in my brain was thrown and I carried on with my work.

*

Just a week or two later, flying at treetop level towards Ruacana from Ondangwa over the open grasslands between Ovamboland and the starkly beautiful Kaokoland, I saw the tell-tale signature of the landmine beast again, about 20 kilometres away and just to the left of the Alo's nose. I reported the explosion to the nearest base by radio and then headed straight for the scene, arriving at the blast site just minutes later.

I came across a Buffel that had detonated a mine. Well, actually, the Buffel had simultaneously detonated three Soviet TM-57 mines, which are shaped like rounds of Gouda cheese, and which had been placed one on top of the other, just in case ten kilograms of high explosive wasn't enough. It was like using a 12-gauge shotgun to swat flies. The occupants of the vehicle, those who were still alive, were writhing grotesquely in the sand in a disorderly ring around the burning wreck.

As I circled around them at a height of a few hundred feet, it seemed to me that they must have been travelling bare-chested at the moment that the mines had exploded, because none of them had on the nutria-brown shirts normally worn by our soldiers. Closer inspection showed that some of them were trouserless too.

The radio crackled into life and someone from the operations room at the nearby base asked whether the injured troops below me were white or black. This really got my back up, as I felt that the skin colour of the troops was immaterial.

'They're our guys!' I shouted into the radio. 'Just get medical help here, asap!'

'Are they black guys or white guys?' the voice persisted.

'They are all white, but what the fuck does that matter?' I spat back.

'We have already dispatched medical people to your location and the casevac choppers are on their way too but we have no white troops in the area,' he responded. 'Are you sure the guys you are looking at are white?'

I was about to erupt with anger and indignation at what I saw as senseless racism but decided first to get a closer view of the casualties. I descended to around 100 feet (30 metres) above the ground, circling the smouldering wreck of the Buffel.

Flip Pretorius and I saw the shocking reality at the same instant.

'They're black guys, Loot,' he said quietly, 'but their skins are burnt off.'

Once again, my automatic switch activated again and numbed my brain.

On Christmas morning 1979 at around 06h00, while all of us Alo crews were dozing in our beds at AFB Ondangwa, contemplating a rare rest day and a substantial feast for lunch, there was a single loud explosion from a distance of about one kilometre away. Since I wasn't that familiar yet with the full range of Border War sounds, my first instinct was to think it was a mortar being fired at us. I braced for the imminent impact and started to plan my escape route to the underground shelter, located a few metres away from the door of our terrapin. But there was no sound of a mortar exploding and I relaxed again.

At breakfast, we were told that a civilian vehicle containing three local Home Guard soldiers, who were travelling to their homes in

Oshakati along the main road from Ondangwa, had detonated three Soviet TM-57 cheese mines laid by PLAN in the tarmac. The explosion, which killed all three men, had occurred just a few hundred metres past the entrance to AFB Ondangwa. It served as a chilling reminder to all of us of the proximity of the conflict to our 'home'.

Consequently, we politely declined any invitations to drive on the roads in the area, even if just to visit the shops in nearby Ondangwa town, citing the oft-repeated excuse that if God had meant for SAAF aircrew to drive or walk on the ground, the colour of the earth would have been blue and not brown.

That Christmas morning also delivered a surprise of infinite personal value to me – a parcel of goodies from my parents. On its own, this was not a rare thing, but the parcel contained a card, handwritten by my mother, which remains one of my most treasured mementos. It was also the last written communication that I would ever get from her. It reads:

Son,
I want you to remember, to never give up no matter what.
I want you to keep going ahead, even if it pains a lot.
I want you to understand, that life can be unfair.
I want you to remember, that I will always be there.
I want you to remember that you could never disappoint me.

At that time, I was quite oblivious to the fact, which was apparent to everyone at home, that my mom deplored my involvement in the Border War. It tore her soul apart every minute that I was in the operational area, and she found it difficult to sleep until I was back home again from my operational tours.

I sailed along, blissfully unaware of her anguish. After the festive season passed, I began to count down the days until my return to 'the States', as we called South Africa, and the European skiing holiday that I'd planned.

*

In the meantime, there was work to be done. At about 11h00 one Saturday morning early in January 1980 the gunships flown by my good friend Brian Bell and I scrambled from Ondangs with orders to get to Ohopoho, the capital of Kaokoland, where we would be given further instructions.

We reached Ohopoho (later called Opuwo) airfield about 80 minutes later, and our flight engineers refuelled while we were briefed on developments by an officer from the local army base. A small convoy comprising two Community Affairs (*Burgersake*) landmine-protected Hippo personnel transport vehicles, which had been tasked with relocating the inhabitants of a village near the border to a safer location further south, had not arrived at its destination as expected. There were also reports of explosions coming from the direction of the convoy.

While Ovamboland is as flat as a pancake, Kaokoland is a mountainous and arid desert landscape with jagged peaks and deep rock-strewn valleys. Water is scarce and few water points exist, all of which are marked on the maps of the area.

Our instructions were to find and secure the convoy and to determine the cause of the delay. We were also told that a senior SADF officer had accompanied the convoy on its journey and that we were to make contact with him if we could. We got airborne and found the convoy within 30 minutes of leaving Ohopoho.

From the air, we could see smoke spiralling upwards. As we approached the scene, we saw that both vehicles were burnt-out. The tyres were still smouldering, accounting for the smoke trails in the sky. The vehicles had obviously stopped for rest and water at one of the map-marked water points. Our attention was attracted by two men, one white and one black, on top of a hill a short distance away. They were waving their arms at us, indicating that we should land.

There were no other signs of life.

We checked the area around the water point thoroughly before landing near the burnt-out Hippos. By this time, the two men had descended from the hilltop and joined us. One was the village headman and the other the senior SADF officer. They told us that the vehicles, carrying all the men, women and children from the village, about 35 souls in total, had stopped for a rest and to replenish their stocks of water at the waterhole. The officer, who was armed only with a hunting rifle, and the headman had decided to climb the hill to get a better view of the starkly beautiful countryside, leaving the rest of the party by the vehicles.

At some point after they reached the hilltop, they noticed unusual activity below. From around 300 metres away they observed a contingent of 40–50 PLAN soldiers surround the vehicle occupants and start to herd them, like cattle, towards the Hippos. The two men, who were unobserved by the PLAN soldiers, immediately sought cover among the rocks.

Shortly afterwards there was the sound of gunfire and several loud explosions.

The PLAN contingent left soon afterwards and the two men remained hidden, knowing that sooner or later there would be an SADF response to the sounds of the attack and to their non-arrival at their planned destination.

'Where are the other villagers now?' we asked.

'They have probably been taken by the PLAN guys. They are known to do this quite often,' replied the officer.

Just then some SADF vehicles and military personnel arrived. The officer and the headman went off to speak to them.

I was curious to see the inside of the still-burning Hippos. As it was impossible to see through the fire-blackened, bullet-resistant glass windows that run the length of both sides of the Hippo, I looked for a place where I could climb onto one of the mudguards without being burnt. I found a foothold, hoisted myself up and peered over the top.

I so wish I had not done that.

The villagers had been crammed into the two Hippos. The doors had then been slammed shut, sealing them all inside.

Then white phosphorous grenades had been tossed in. Some of the occupants had tried to escape the 1 000 °C-plus inferno by squeezing through the gap between the walls of the Hippo and its roof but had been shot by the animals waiting outside.

I stared at the contorted shapes of the charred bodies of the villagers filling the back of the vehicle. The scene was as horrific as any I'd ever seen in photos of Nazi concentration camps. Wide-eyed and uncomprehending, I found it impossible to move for at least a few seconds, possibly even a minute or two.

The final image, forever etched into my brain, was that of the faintly recognisable skeletons of a mother and her suckling child, with the child's skull still fused to her mum's sternum.

Then, thankfully, the switch in my brain activated again, immediately damping, then halting, and finally deflating the explosive deluge of primeval and raw rage that threatened to overwhelm me.

Somehow, I managed to step off the Hippo's mudguard and walk away.

*

The sleep deprivation resulting from all my late-night confrontations with the day's events in my bed under my mosquito net was somewhat blunted by my heavy consumption of quantities of pink gin and tonic. This was the drink of choice for chopper crews, simply because at ten cents an imperial tot of Beefeater gin with Indian tonic and a dash of Angostura bitters, it cost substantially less than a can of beer (25 cents).

Late one night around a fire in the aircrew living area at Ondangwa, midnight was beckoning. A handful of chopper pilots, some new, some not so new – all young – were sitting around the dying embers of the fire. The conversation gravitated, as it always did at that time of each G&T-fuelled night, to the possibility of dying. Not surprisingly, this undesirable scenario was considered by most of us to be a quite distinct probability, given where we found ourselves.

The quinine-laced Indian tonic in the G&Ts had, as usual, thoroughly depressed the drinkers, and the atmosphere at the fireside was morose and introspective. Soon, one by one, everyone would quietly leave the fire and make their way to their beds, crawl under their mosquito nets and try to get some sleep before the anaesthetic effect of the gin wore off and, in the pre-dawn light, their flight engineers would bring steaming mugs of *moerkoffie* (filter coffee) to the groggy flyers, heralding the start of another day.

'We all know that when it's your time to go, it's your time to go! Get over it!' one of the group said.

'If the fucking bullet comes up at you with your name and address on the front, there's bugger all you can do about it!' growled an ouman. 'So why worry about it?'

Heads nodded in agreement and silence prevailed for a few seconds.

Then, just as the first pilot rose to his feet to leave, or to vomit into a nearby flowerbed, a gravelly voice, speaking slower than BJ Vorster addressing a Republic Day rally, uttered these unforgettable words:

'Gentlemen … I … completely agree … that there is … sweet … fuck all … that I can do … about the bullet … that has my name … and my address … on it. So … I lose no sleep … over it.'

Drawing a deep breath, he went on: 'But the bullet … that makes me … kak myself … each minute … of each hour … of each day … that I fly in this fucking war … is the one addressed … "To whom it may concern".'

6

Thinking about escape

And then, quite anticlimactically, my first stint on the Border was over and I boarded the Flossie for the three-hour flight back to AFB Waterkloof in Pretoria. I had only been there for about three months, but I had already seen and experienced much more than any young man would be exposed to under normal circumstances.

Waiting in the arrivals hall that Thursday evening were my mom and dad. But, tanned as I was, and with my wildly long hair bleached bright blond by the Ovamboland sun, and my sunburnt cheeks bloated from excessive consumption of G&T, they both looked directly at me but walked past me twice.

'Mom, Dad, it's me!' I exclaimed as they threatened to pass me by a third time and I removed the military-issue brown floppy hat from my head to dispel all doubt.

My mom turned towards the sound of my voice, and then, seeing where it came from, her eyes immediately grew to the size of saucers and she burst into tears, folding me into those graceful arms of her and squeezing me so tight that I thought I'd break.

'What have those bastards done to him?' she hissed at my dad over my shoulder. 'He's just a child.'

In a concerted effort to avoid an incident, my dad and I guided my mom from the arrivals hall to the privacy of their car. All the way during the 45-minute journey back to the Wonderboom farm, my mom never took her eyes off me. She seemed to examine every pore, every strand of hair and every freckle to make sure they were all still there.

The intensity of her attention was quite disconcerting. Her mouth kept opening, as if to ask a question, but then would close again without her saying anything. She stared intently into my eyes, looking, I think, for something recognisable, something familiar.

Now that I have children of my own I realise that she was probably trying to see inside my head, to see if she could spot the damage she suspected was hidden there. If she could identify it, she probably thought she could do something to heal the wounds and the shattered innocence and make me whole again, like I'd been when I'd left for the Border just three months before.

As my mother was busy inspecting me, I had a vague sense that perhaps something fundamental had changed in me, but I couldn't yet put my finger on what exactly. On reaching the farm I made a cursory attempt to probe the actual cause of the shift in my alignment but found that my concentration quickly waned. I was far more comfortable dealing with the mundane, everyday things that a returning soldier might pursue, such as where to party the night away, who to do it with and whether there was petrol in my car.

So, I called up the Boytjie from Benoni and told him I was home for a day or two. He and a group of friends were going to the Grand Wazoo that evening and he suggested that I join them.

My mom had prepared a special welcome-home meal for me and was noticeably irritated when I wolfed down the exquisitely cooked rump steak and trimmings, dived into the shower and emerged a short while later ready for an extended night on the town.

'Where are you going?' she asked.

'Out,' I replied.

'Where are you going out to?'

'To a club.'

'Who are you going with?'

'Friends.'

'When will you be home?'

'Later.'

Miffed, she turned to my dad and whispered, 'Please ask him to give us details. You know how dangerous it is for young people travelling alone at night around Pretoria lately!'

My dad just stood up, wrapped his arms around her and hugged her tightly.

*

Two days after leaving Ondangwa, I boarded a British Airways Boeing 747 at Jan Smuts Airport (now OR Tambo International Airport), bound for London.

One of the positives about ops tours of a mostly predetermined time span was that my entire monthly overhead ceased and I could comfortably live on the R3 per day danger allowance that I drew at the AFB Ondangwa paymaster's office every week or so. This was more than enough to keep me in drinks and cigarettes while on operational duty.

It also meant that my full salary was banked back home and that I could calculate the exact amount I'd have available upon my return from the tour. Before leaving for the Border, I had handed a travel agent friend my passport and my building society savings book and asked her to book me on a European skiing holiday and to arrange all the necessary visas and traveller's cheques.

The day after my homecoming, I popped into her office and she gave me my itinerary. I was to leave the next evening. I would stay in London for four days in a nice hotel in South Kensington while the other 15-odd members of our touring party assembled at the same hotel from around the globe. Four days later we would fly to Munich and then travel by coach into the Stubaital, a picturesque valley in Austria, where we would spend two and a half weeks at a hotel in Neustift-im-Stubaital, skiing the days away.

At the end of the Neustift stay, we would coach back to Munich and fly to Amsterdam for three days before I returned to Johannesburg via London. The total price of the trip, excluding my spending money, was the princely sum of R1 470.

I calculated that my next ops tour would start just three days after I returned to South Africa, so the timing was inch-perfect.

I didn't sleep a wink on the flight and, like a real country bumpkin, sampled everything I could. The drinks were on the house too. Arriving in London on a typically murky, cloudy and rainy Sunday morning did nothing to dampen either my exuberance or my energy, and I set about exploring the city, on my own, just minutes after checking into my hotel.

My first port of call was to surprise an old friend, Jeremy Lyons, who had moved to London a few years previously and was working as a manager for McDonald's, his mother had told me. I'd walked no more than 500 metres from my hotel and there, right in front of me, was McDonald's. I couldn't believe my luck.

In the restaurant, I went up to the first available assistant, a tall, dreadlocked Caribbean woman.

'Is Jeremy Lyons here?' I asked.

'Jeremy who, mon?' she responded in a smooth and husky West Indian lilt.

'Jeremy Lyons, he's the manager here,' I said authoritatively.

'No brother, Jackie Scuttlebone is the manager here. Are you sure you have the right place, mon?' she asked doubtfully.

'Yes, his mother told me just two days ago that he is the manager at McDonald's in London!'

'There are 27 McDonald's branches in London, mon!' she replied. 'Which one is he in?'

'One of the others,' I said sheepishly and quickly left the restaurant.

Back at the hotel, I hooked up with one of the other members of our tour. I was keen to see an X-rated movie, something South Africans who'd never travelled internationally before had only heard about in hushed conversations in all-male company. We went to see *Mad Max*, starring a very young Mel Gibson. But the only sex scene, if you could even call it that, and which I naturally associated with the X-rating, was a second or two of sodomy filmed from a great distance. However, the gratuitous violence in the post-apocalyptic world of *Mad Max* began with the opening scene and was still going at full tilt when the credits rolled at the end of the film. Violence was the last thing that I had travelled 15 000 kilometres to encounter.

Our group grew larger as new members arrived and we booked tickets for the rock opera *Jesus Christ Superstar*, which was banned in South Africa at the time as being 'scandalous blasphemy' of the worst kind. One of the new arrivals was Angie, who was from somewhere on the Gold Coast of Australia. She immediately attracted the close scrutiny and attention of every fellow in the group as she was built like a Playboy model (I didn't know what that meant, but the other, less-hillbilly guys explained).

On the evening of the performance, she arrived in the foyer of our hotel, where we were gathering before leaving for the Odeon Theatre, dressed in the tightest-fitting pair of denim jeans in global history.

Quite innocently, I asked, 'Jeez Angie, how in blazes name do you get into those jeans?'

'Well, mate, you start by buying me a drink!' she said.

The vacuum resulting from the instantaneous headlong rush to the bar by the tour's masculine contingent nearly created a hole in the space-time continuum.

Four days later we flew to Munich and spent the day travelling from pub to pub quaffing significant quantities of Weissbier (wheat beer), as planned. Understandably, none of us recalled much of the three-hour coach journey from Munich to Neustift-im-Stubaital later that evening.

I woke up the next morning feeling thick-headed (more so than usual) in what turned out to be a delightfully cosy and hospitable little Gasthaus (inn) located right on the edge of the main square of Neustift. The town was situated at the bottom of the Stubaital. The valley floor appeared to rise gently before suddenly towering steeply upwards to where the Stubai glacier began its frozen tumble down from the top of its 4 000-metre-high Alpine source. The lower reaches of a renowned ski run called the Schlick wound their insanely precipitous way down through the trees on the mountainside directly opposite my vantage point. I could see the minute figures of expert skiers hurtling down its crazy slopes even though it was still early in the morning.

In the square below me, groups of novice skiers, carrying their skis on their shoulders, dressed in padded suits and multicoloured woollen beanies, were waiting for a bus to take them up the valley to the cableway station at the foot of the Stubai glacier for a day of carefree fun and frolicking in the snow and ice. It struck me that the most critical decision I would make that day would probably be related to what I was going to order to eat, and that the situation from which I'd been extracted just a week before could not have been more different from where I now found myself.

For the first few days, all of us novices attended a training course on the baby slopes within the confines of the village, designed specifically to equip beginners with sufficient skills to prevent us from falling on the icy paths between the various village pubs and our respective hotels. Only once those initial skills had been absorbed and demonstrated to the satisfaction of skiing instructors would we be let loose on the ski slopes proper. Part of the instruction was learning to fall without incurring crippling injuries.

I fell down.

I fell down a great deal, sometimes while skiing, and it is inarguable testimony to the expert tutelage of the skiing instructors that I am still alive today.

At the beginning of our stay in Neustift, our tour overlapped for two days with one run by the same company that was coming to an end after being based in the village for more than a fortnight. In the outgoing tour party were five Rhodesian chaps. I was told by reliable sources that the Rhodies had done everything in their power, 24 hours a day, for the past two weeks, to drink the Stubaital dry. They were quite easy to identify, as they always wore

T-shirts over whatever else they'd donned that day. The T-shirts had 'Advice to every terrorist' on the front and 'Go fuck yourself before we do!' on the back.

Being the only person from Africa in my tour party, I felt duty-bound to introduce myself to these fellow southern Africans and to buy them all a beer. I also hoped to glean some important information from them regarding local conditions, such as the best pubs and clubs, dos and don'ts of a general nature, and where best to make contact with the ladies.

'Fuck, man,' slurred the first Rhodie, 'even the fucking shithouses have fucking pubs in them! Go any-fucking-where, the bastard motherfuckers who created this shithole made sure that it's fucking great!'

The second said something along the lines of 'We have only fucking been arrested four fucking times by those cock-sucking Gestapo police pricks since we fucking got here, but I can't fucking remember why so there aren't that many fucking rules here, I think!'

The third, obviously a keener observer than the others, said, 'There are shitloads of arse-puckering, fucking gorgeous fucking women wherever you look, but they keep on fucking running away when we fucking want to talk to them about shagging! Fucking stuck-up bitches, wouldn't know a red-blooded African prong if you rubbed the fucking thing against them in a fucking cable car!'

The Rhodies invited me to have a farewell drink with them, so I met up with them in a nearby pub. The paint-peelingly vulgar, profanity-rich (but very descriptive) conversation, together with a thick cloud of smoke from chain-smoked Madison cigarettes, soon had patrons from adjacent tables moving away in search of clearer air.

Just then, Richarde, the Rhodies' skiing instructor, walked into the pub and joined us, having also been invited to toast the imminent departure of the Boys from Bulawayo. Dangling on his arm, seemingly attached to it like a limpet mine, was the most stunningly gorgeous, radiantly sensual, auburn-haired beauty in the town. He introduced her as Gundie, and in seconds I was smitten.

Now, before you get the wrong idea and condemn me for flippancy and shallowness, please bear in mind that I was not, at this stage, nor for a long time to come, functioning at an optimum emotional level. There was nothing wrong with my senses of sight, sound, touch, smell or taste, however. They were operating well, but the depth to which I was able to explore my emotions was limited, to say the least. Consequently, saying that I was 'smitten' was absolutely true, at least for that time.

Gundie chose to get as far away from the rowdy quintet of Rhodesian bush people as was possible at an eight-seater table, and ended up sitting next to me. As she spoke passable English and I could mumble the odd German-sounding phrase, we immediately struck up a pleasant conversation and connected as if we'd known each other for some time.

Before too long she suggested that we remove ourselves to the dance floor situated in the next room. I was a little uncomfortable with this proposal, fearing that I would be perceived by Richarde to be 'moving in' on his territory. Ever an advocate for preventive maintenance, I asked Richarde if he had any objections to my dancing with his girlfriend. He laughed aloud and said, 'My friend, Gundie is just an acquaintance. The night is young and the available *mädchen* endless. Please have fun in Neustift. That is why it is here!'

From then on, I began to seriously like Neustift and its friendly inhabitants.

*

A day or two later, as I stood waiting nervously at the edge of the village square for the glacier-bound public bus to arrive, with my skis perched on my right shoulder like everyone else seemed to be doing, a sizeable crowd of skiers with the same obvious intentions as me gathered at the bus stop.

When the bus arrived, everyone rushed forward in a manner reminiscent of a buffalo stampede, inexplicably eager to be the first to board the bus and stand next to their skis for the 45 minutes it would take to reach the lower cableway station at the foot of the Stubai glacier. Someone needed to take action to prevent injury or, worse still, loss of life, and so I forced my two-metre-long skis into a horizontal barrier, effectively bringing the headlong rush for the bus door to a halt.

Then, in my best German, I commanded, '*Halten Sie! Alten Damen ... eerste!*'

The first four words, *Halten Sie!* (Stop!) and *alten Damen* (old ladies), were proper German words, but *eerste* (first) was Afrikaans.

The crowd, to my amazement, complied with my instruction and five or six ladies of more advanced years boarded solemnly. None thanked me for my chivalry. Then, meaning to say, 'Now the younger ladies', I suddenly realised in a panic that my limited German vocabulary didn't stretch that far. So I said, with all the authority and brevity that I could muster, '*Nun, die jungen Frauen!*'

To my astonishment, ten or so young ladies detached themselves from the stunned crowd and climbed the stairs onto the bus. The first nine didn't even acknowledge me, but the tenth, whose derriere I was lecherously ogling as she boarded, did. As she reached the top of the stairs she turned around to me and said, 'Thank you, kind sir. Thank you very much.'

For the second time in the past 72 hours, I was totally smitten. I was absolutely certain that this vision of perfection must be Jacqueline Bisset, the beautiful English actress whom I'd loved passionately for years since seeing her, five times, as the pregnant air hostess in *Airport*, or at least her identical twin sister.

Her name, however, was Atie Hofstra and she was from Rotterdam.

I was suddenly floating, dazed. I banged my shins only twice on the steel steps in the stairwell as I followed Atie at what I imagined to be a discreet distance as she looked for a vacant perch, until she stopped to sit down and I clattered into her. Her blonde-framed head snapped around, momentarily irked by the klutzical (but completely unintentional and barely discernible) collision of my head with the small of her back. But then, seeing it was me, her expression immediately softened and she gestured for me to share the seat with her.

Atie was in her late twenties and worked as an international exchange operator at the European Telephone Exchange in Rotterdam. She was also a recruiter for Amnesty International, which happened to be an organisation that didn't much like what my employer, the SADF, was doing in southern Africa. Amnesty International was also actively and intensively involved in the burgeoning global anti-apartheid movement. Thus, the groundwork was laid for a brief and electrically charged relationship between a beautiful and unapologetic idealist on the one side and a transient and careless temporary combat escapee on the other.

From that first moment, Atie subjected me to a never-ending barrage of questions. Interested, intelligent and considered questions, which, for me to answer even at a surface level, required that I look below the veneer at who I was, and what I would continue to be involved with, when I returned home in just a few short weeks.

I instinctively sensed that this was an arena that I didn't have the slightest interest in entering, but I also sensed that revealing my mindset honestly to Atie would have jeopardised our relationship, something to which I was even more averse. So, her unrelenting drive for answers and my determined dodging of her questions – a 24-hour-a-day game of cut and thrust, countered by parry and block – became the order of the day in the Stubaital for the next week.

Sleep became superfluous as we skied the days away. Atie was a real expert and a talented tutor and passed on to me a wealth

My Dutch friend Atie and me, after a hard day's skiing in Austria.

of winter sport skills that largely prevented me from falling more than one or two thousand times a day.

Such was the intensity of our interaction that one moment we would be gliding along laughing uproariously at some antic or other and the next she'd be pelting me with snowballs from frustration at my eluding her latest probing inquiry. It would particularly infuriate her when she'd ask a penetrating question aimed at revealing some emotion I was suppressing, according to her, and I'd evade by 'singing' the Beatles' 'We all live in a mellow submarine!' or 'Eight ways a week!' at the top of my voice.

I was sitting at a bar counter one evening, waiting for her to join me, when a complete stranger sat down next to me and engaged me in conversation. I noticed that he had a southern African accent. He said that he was the owner of a tour company in the area, was originally Rhodesian, and had moved to Innsbruck five years previously. He seemed to know quite a bit about me, which I found a little odd but put it down to the fact that I'd been in Neustift for about a week at that stage and hadn't been shy in engaging with locals and tourists alike.

He quickly got to the point. He 'strongly advised' me to consider coming to work for his company in Austria and abandoning my life back home. He went on to say, correctly, that South Africa was becoming a pariah state, and that my personal involvement in the SADF would not stand me in good stead in the future.

He suggested that, if I looked at things carefully, I would see that my visit to Neustift could be viewed in the same light as St Paul's epiphany on the road to Damascus. I knew who St Paul was, but I didn't know what the true meaning of 'epiphany' was. I thought it meant 'gift'. As a consequence, our conversation began to go downhill. As is my nature when I am nervous or unsettled, and to hide my ignorance, I told him a joke about St Paul meeting a drunk and driving him home. Irritated and exasperated by what he must have perceived as my disinterest and flippancy, he left. It was only many years later that I began to wonder if there was perhaps a connection between Atie and him ...

*

The day after Atie left to go back home to Rotterdam, our tour leader invited all the members of the tour to attend an *après-ski* (after-ski) cocktail party for a visiting group of South African travel agents who were passing through Neustift.

The conditions in an Austrian ski resort in early 1980 were the absolute antithesis of those on the Border. As such, it would seem reasonable to assume that there could surely not be any possible connection between the two places, situated as they were many thousands of kilometres apart.

As I walked into the gathering, still suffering from a degree of separation-from-Atie anxiety, I was instantly drawn to, and locked eyes with, a beautiful woman standing across the room. Her long curly auburn hair caught the last beams of the setting sun filtering through the window. She was a vision of loveliness.

Trying desperately to regain my composure and not fluff my unrehearsed lines, I made my way across to her and introduced myself. Within seconds, the world and the people surrounding the two of us ceased to exist as we became engrossed in one another's presence. How long we stood there, oblivious to the outside world, I do not know. Then, at the outer peripherals of both my vision and my hearing, I became vaguely aware that the tour leader had located a microphone and had begun to address the attendees. After welcoming the visitors, he introduced the members of our touring party to the travel agents.

'Over there,' he said pointing out the individuals one by one 'is Deborah, an accountant from Toronto, Canada. And to her left with the red Heidi-hat is Willy, a farmer from Auckland, New Zealand.'

I was drowning in my newfound soul mate's spectacular eyes, and was still only vaguely aware of the proceedings, when the tour leader said, 'And there, with that moggy grin on his face is Steve, an Air Force helicopter pilot from Pretoria, South Africa!'

I vividly recall how she jumped back, as if I'd struck her, and stood glaring murderously at me. Then, finding her voice, she screamed, 'You're a *what?*'

All conversation in the room instantly ceased, and before I had the chance to answer, the stunned tour leader stammered, 'He's a ... a S-S-S ... South African Air Force chopper pilot.'

'Do you know Gary Harper[1]?' screeched my rapidly retreating dream girl at me.

'What's he got to do with things?' was all I could muster, perplexed by her mention of a chopper pilot colleague with whom I had a vague acquaintance.

'Do you know Gary?' she spat, snarled and hissed at me, all at the same time.

'Barely,' I replied. 'Our bush tours overlapped for a week or two,' I said truthfully, confusion etched on my face.

At that moment, I was willing to go to the ends of the earth to describe the gulf of distance between said Gary and me, if it

---

1   A pseudonym.

could in any way rescue a situation that was rapidly slipping out of control.

'YOU ... you chopper bastards are all the same!' she exploded.

Those were the last words she uttered directly to me as her friends and colleagues quickly gathered around her, like a laager of Voortrekker wagons, and escorted her from the venue. Try as I might over the next 24 hours, there was no piercing the impenetrable wall of steel thrown up around her and getting her to hear me out.

A day later she moved on to her next destination and I was left in a small Austrian resort town, devastated. All I was able to determine later on was that she came from Port Elizabeth, had encountered Gary, and didn't ever send him Christmas cards.

*

The Netherlands was the final stop on the tour. At Schipol Airport in Amsterdam, after I had made my way through immigration and customs, I became aware of an insistent drumming on the glass partition coming from the side of the arrivals hall. When I looked up to see the source, I looked straight into the eyes of Atie.

Some quick rearrangements with the local tour operator ensued, and before I knew it, Atie whisked me off to her car, a sporty little Mercedes, and we were on the freeway heading for Rotterdam and her home, where I was to stay for the duration of the Dutch leg of my holiday. After meeting Atie's mother, who lived with her, she and I went to a pub-restaurant to meet with a group of her friends.

Before leaving South Africa, I had been warned by colleagues, friends and even members of my own family to expect extreme hostility from almost everyone I would meet on my foreign travels. The prevailing opinion was that South Africa, and everything that was happening in the country, was completely misrepresented by the foreign media, and that the people I would encounter would almost certainly be aggressive, misinformed, judgemental and possibly even violent.

In fact, I was told, it was incomprehensible that anyone who loved South Africa would subject themselves to this type of punishment. I must be insane to fork out my hard-earned money to travel to these climes, where I would be under constant threat. I think the irony may have escaped them.

By the time I met Atie's friends, I had not yet met anyone who wanted to take my head off or to charge me for my manifold sins at the International Court of Justice, which, incidentally, we drove past in Den Haag en route from Amsterdam to Rotterdam. From the moment I was introduced, Atie's friends inundated me with questions, not a single one of which had even the slightest hint of enmity. Their interest in South Africa, its people, its natural beauty, its wildlife, its resources, its history and its future, was insatiable. They also seemed interested in me, and I got a hint of what it must be like to enjoy (mild) celebrity status.

At no point was the subject of apartheid directly raised, yet, in hindsight, it was the proverbial elephant in the room. In any event, I had never been stupid enough to try and defend it. I rationalised my involvement in the SADF as a necessary, even vital, stepping-stone to a career in the aviation industry, as my parents simply lacked the financial means to pay for me to become a commercial pilot.

As the evening wore on, the circle of friends shrunk until finally there were only four of us – Atie, me and a married couple called Kurt and Inge.

The conversation gradually turned to probing my short- and medium-term future. What plans did I have? Did I see my future in South Africa? What was a future South Africa going to look like? What role would I play, if any? What were the economic prospects for me, for the country and for the southern African region? Was I going to get married, have children? Where would I live? Was there even a future for me in South Africa?

I could not remember when last, if ever, I had taken the time or made the effort to explore these aspects of my existence. To my hosts, I must surely have appeared like a deer caught in the headlights of an oncoming car. They also wouldn't let me simply dodge the myriad questions posed, as I had become quite expert at doing, and kept gently nudging me back into the discomfort that often results from self-reflection.

At some point the suggestion was made that I consider staying on in the Netherlands and not return to South Africa, as planned, a few days hence. I immediately dismissed the notion, citing the undeniable fact that my finances were dwindling rapidly. Babbling on, I told them that I did not relish the thought of enduring the Dutch winter on the streets, homeless, and that I also feared the repercussions for my family back home should I desert the SADF. As far as I knew, desertion was still a punishable offence and my parents and siblings would likely be the ones to feel the effects of my actions. My mother, who held quite a senior management position at the CSIR, would be particularly vulnerable to the consequences of the choices I made far from home.

They said that I should not consider lack of money to be a problem, as that could be taken care of, as could accommodation and employment. Their proposal was that I should seek asylum in the Netherlands. This response, I suspect with the wisdom of hindsight, was anything but impulsive, and the possibility should have occurred to me that a well-constructed and considered plan was being carefully played out. Their proposal was made just a little too quickly for it to have been a late-night, spur-of-the-moment thing.

But still, it got me thinking, and think I did.

The next day, Atie, playing the role of the world's most attractive tour guide, took me all over the country, showing me the delights and consequences of the hard-won battle to reclaim the land from the North Sea. I became an instant fan of the Dutch people.

All day long I considered the previous evening's proposal, and by the time we got back to Rotterdam, the outlines of a plan had started to take root. I told Atie that if I could cash my last traveller's cheque and convert my return air ticket into cash, I would probably have enough to pay my way for the short while it would take for me to declare myself a refugee and be granted asylum by the Dutch government and finalise arrangements for gainful employment.

She seemed ecstatic with the direction of my thinking and we agreed to put the plan into action in Amsterdam the next day.

That night she took me to a Russian bar in the back streets of Rotterdam. It was rather a disconcerting environment for me, an innocent young fellow from Pretoria, who'd been raised with the notion that the Soviet Union was the epitome of all that was evil in the world.

After an 'interesting' meal consisting of numerous variations of red cabbage, accompanied by a fat-congealed conglomeration of protein of questionable origins, and washed down with miniature glasses of eye-poppingly potent vodka, the primary purpose of the visit to this little piece of the Soviet Union was revealed. I was introduced to an absolute giant of a man, whose name may have been Igor or Alexey or Ivan.

He sported a Paul Kruger-like beard that reached all the way to his navel and a leather jacket-and-shirt combo surely made from the hides of two mammoths. His hands could easily have crushed icebergs and were just as cold to the touch. An odd bearlike growl seemed to emanate straight out of the middle of this giant's ample chest.

He sat down opposite me and just stared at me, unblinking, for a full two minutes. If his aim was to intimidate me, he succeeded. A fine film of perspiration oozed from every pore on my petrified face. His mouth opened, but only slightly, and he started speaking.

Atie translated.

'He wants to know why you are fighting his friends in Angola.'

'Uh … Tell him it's not me doing that. It must be the other guys,' I said in my most convincing voice.

'He says you are talking bullshit. He has the names of every enemy pilot there and you are one of them.'

'Oh ... In that case, please tell him I'm thinking of leaving. I never really liked it there.'

Silence.

After an interminable wait, Rasputin's bigger nephew growled:

'Will you go in front of the press and tell them that what South Africa is doing in Angola is wrong?'

'I will think about it ... Can we please go now?' I pleaded with Atie.

'He wants to know when you'll decide.'

'Tomorrow?' I offered timidly.

'He is happy with that. But now he wants you to have a drink with him to seal the deal.'

Even if I'd had any choice of who to drink with at that moment, which I didn't, my knees were knocking so hard, and my legs were so jelly-like, that I couldn't have walked away if you'd held a gun to my head. So we drank, like old friends, into the wee small hours until some kind soul got me home and put me to bed ... but I'd still not stopped shitting myself – figuratively speaking, of course.

I woke early that Friday morning.

I lay in bed and tried manfully to sort out the conflicting emotions raging in my head. Life had been so easy up to that point, the choices simple, the parameters crisp and clear, the routines set and predictable. Now I was seemingly committed to following through on some quite heady stuff.

Desertion ... asylum ... persecution and prosecution?

Shit, I thought, as the cogs in my brain spun and then threatened to smash against each other. If I went public, as the Russian wanted, I might even become the target of South African assassins. It had happened before.

While these were things I could still handle, what about those who'd be caught in the crossfire, particularly the members of my family? My mom's hard-won position at the CSIR aside, my sister had recently become engaged to a senior Foreign Affairs diplomat, and I doubted that she'd be unaffected. My brother was doing his national service and many of my dad's friends were SADF military people.

Feeling conflicted, I packed my backpack and Atie and I went to Amsterdam. On the way, we debated the first port of call and I was adamant that it be the local British Airways office, so that I might generate the available funds to complete the initial phase of the plan.

I really don't know if I would have gone through with the plan had British Airways cooperated, but the entire process was halted when the airline personnel refused point-blank to refund the money for my return ticket. I made an obligatory, but small, scene about being a frequent flyer (true for the past month) and stated my disgust at their uncooperative attitude. But deep down I already knew that the damage my decision to seek asylum in the Netherlands would have wrought on my loved ones was a lot more than I was willing to accept responsibility for.

Atie was devastated by my capitulation, which she saw as a convenient excuse to return to my comfort zone rather than to make an honourable but irreversible stand. She urged, and then begged, me to go to the Dutch interior ministry and put myself at their mercy. At one point, she dashed into a bank and emerged with a sizeable wad of cash that she tried to thrust into my hands and pockets, insisting that money, or my lack thereof, was temporary and should be no obstacle to my 'doing the right thing'.

She tried wailing loudly, attracting a lot of attention from passers-by. The battle raged for the entire morning, up and down the streets that we walked along. Around lunchtime, as we were walking down a little road next to a canal, she suddenly looked up and told me to stay where I was as she had a surprise for me. She dashed across the road to a mobile sandwich vendor.

A few minutes later she returned, carrying something in her hand. She handed me the parcel and said, 'This is a typical Dutch sandwich. I think you might know it as steak tartare.'

I unfolded the wrapper, revealing an open baguette covered from one end to the other with what looked like raw mince. On top of the mince were the yolks of three raw chicken eggs.

'Eat it,' Atie ordered.

'It's a bit underdone, even for my liking,' I replied sceptically, raising an eyebrow.

'Then just taste it, please, Steve. Do that one thing for me?' she pleaded sweetly, and I knew that I had to comply.

As I lifted the concoction to my mouth, Atie stepped in front of me and, using both her hands for leverage, slammed the uncooked and gooey mess into my face as hard as she could. I was blinded by the sticky mixture of raw beef and egg yolk covering my face, ears included. I stood rooted to the spot in shock and surprise at the violence and suddenness of the assault.

I tried to clear my eyes but the next moment Atie stepped forward and shoved her compact mirror directly into my field of vision and screamed, 'What do you see?'

'What do you mean?' I hissed back 'You've just ruined my only clean shirt!'

Thrusting the mirror even closer to my face made me squint and draw back but also revealed the reflection of a face that looked like it'd been through the blades of a rotary lawnmower running at full speed.

She shouted, 'That's what your guns do to people, you … you murdering bastard!'

It took some time for the words to sink in. As I stood there trying vainly to clean myself up, Atie continued to rant and rave. After a while she just stopped shouting and stood there, glaring fiercely at me while I picked little flecks of meat from my eyebrows and forelock. The sandwich vendor, who'd been observing the proceedings closely, and deducing that it was safe to approach, came over with a damp cloth to help me wipe away the remaining muck.

Looking at Atie, as her anger and indignation slowly leached away and the tension between us waned, and still astounded by the vehemence of her outburst, I felt a range of emotions well up inside me. My newfound doubts about the morality of my SADF involvement, my regret at the anguish I was causing to those close to me, and my trepidation at what the future held for me, brought tears to my eyes. But, summoning all the strength I had, I managed to choke them down and slam the lids on those cans of worms.

Then, in a rare encounter with clarity, consideration and vision, I said softly, 'Atie, if I don't go back, the consequences for my family and others will be bad. There's a right way to get out and it isn't ... like this.'

Atie's grudging acceptance of my rationale, and the release of the immense pressure that had built up between us, made the declaration of a truce possible.

Although Atie tried, many times, to visit me in South Africa, she was always denied a visa for some reason. Later, the intervals between when we spoke on the telephone, or wrote to each other, gradually grew further and further apart, until the relationship finally petered out completely.

7

The day my world changed

Back in South Africa, I barely had time to repack my battered old kitbag before I found myself on a Flossie headed for Ondangwa for a one-month tour.

Within days of my arrival I participated in a fresh operation with helicopter aircrews based at New Etale, just a kilometre or two from the infamous Oshikango Gate border post. The role of the four gunships stationed there was to be on stand-by to provide close air support to a company of troops who were going to be dropped about 30 kilometres inside Angola, tasked with finding and destroying a PLAN base that had recently been established in the area.

My wingman and I had spent the previous night at Nkongo, 120 kilometres east of New Etale, and we only arrived well after the commencement of the operation and as the second or third wave of troop-carrying Puma helicopters headed across the cutline and towards the landing zone inside enemy territory.

Two gunships flown, respectively, by Chris Stroebel and his wingman Billy Fourie, were already circling the drop zone to prevent any surprise attack from the enemy as the vulnerable Pumas came into land and disgorged the troops they were carrying. I had just made myself comfortable against some sandbags in the ops room when the VHF radio on the table next to me crackled into life and the faint voice of another Puma co-pilot, Steve Erasmus, said, 'We have contact! There are lots of them. We are being *looied* (lashed)!'

Dead silence followed and immediately all ears tuned to the radio.

The radio crackled again and the same co-pilot came on: 'My commander has been hit. We are turning back and going to Oshakati.'

His words were barely out and we were running for our gunships.

Fifteen minutes later we reached the point of contact, where Chris and Billy were already engaged with a sizeable force on the ground and were taking heavy fire.

The arrival of two more gunships must have tipped the balance and the enemy soldiers quickly melted into the thick bush and disappeared, probably into a network of tunnels. As we circled the area we noticed tendrils of white smoke regularly spiralling up into the sky around us, but didn't think much more about them other than to report their appearance in the post-ops debriefing when we got back to Ondangwa later that evening.

During that night, every member of the chopper crews who'd been at New Etale the previous day came down with a severe case of 'gyppo guts' (gastroenteritis). Through the night and into the early morning, one by one, we all ended up being carried into the Ondangwa sickbay and hooked up to drips. My engineer and I were the last to succumb, and the doctors put this down to our later arrival at New Etale.

An investigation into the cause of this sudden illness revealed that a local inhabitant of Ovamboland had managed to make his way through the flimsy security fence surrounding New Etale's 15-metre-deep well, dug specifically to supply the base with potable drinking water, and had fallen into the well and drowned. Over a few days, or possibly even a few weeks, his body had begun to decompose and contaminate the water in the process.

In the aftermath of that macabre news, it was difficult to consume any water, so we stuck to canned carbonated drinks during the day and gin and tonic in the evening.

A few days after the operation against the PLAN base, all aircrews were invited to attend a briefing by the ops intelligence people in the Ondangwa briefing room. Billy Fourie, normally a highly vocal character and an experienced Impala instructor at FTS Langebaanweg, was married with children. He had only recently finished his conversion to Alo IIIs and was on his first bush tour. Since the events of a few days before, Billy had said almost nothing to anyone, which was most unusual for him, but, because everyone responds differently to combat conditions, this didn't even raise a comment.

In the ops intelligence briefings at Ondangs, we'd normally receive feedback on odd things that we'd reported during missions, new developments and assessments would be discussed, and information that could affect our mission success was divulged. I was not paying close attention to the presentation until I heard the intelligence officer mention the tendrils of white smoke that we'd reported. Almost nonchalantly he said, 'Those white smoke spirals that you gunship crews reported appearing in the sky around you near Chiede a few days ago were from SAM-7s (surface-to-air missiles), chaps. The terrs have upgraded their weaponry again.'

Nothing more. Just that.

I was still wrapping my head around what he'd said, and whether there was anything more to be discussed about this scary new threat, when Billy Fourie stood up and said vehemently, 'Fuck this. Fuck this war. I am not prepared to die here. I have a wife and kids. You can shove your fucking war!' and then stomped noisily out of the room, away from Ondangs and ultimately out of the SAAF.

At the time, like most of the other pilots there, I was stunned that a fellow pilot could just walk out like that, abandoning his mates and his career. However, as it didn't affect me directly, I moved on unperturbed, as, it seemed, did everyone else. While it wasn't exactly a taboo subject, we spoke little about it in the days, weeks and months that followed.

A short while later, an Impala pilot, whose name eludes me, did the same thing.

It was only years later, long after I'd left the SAAF and when my own cans of worms had mostly been opened and neatly processed under the expert guidance of a professional psychologist, that I realised what enormous strength and courage it took for Billy Fourie, and for the other guy, to turn away from convention and face the punishing consequences of their decisions.

*

A week or so before the end of my tour, I was flying one of two gunships tasked with providing top cover to a gaggle of Pumas doing a troop drop close to Vila Roçadas, where the near-disaster caused by the outdated hand-drawn map had occurred just a few months before.

This time, using better navigation skills and improved cartography, the drop went smoothly and all the aircraft involved departed the scene and headed southwards for the border. The groundspeed of the Alo III being far slower than that of the Puma meant that the two gunships were left a long way behind, and we followed our own route back to Ruacana, where we were due to refuel.

For no more reason than a change of scenery, we opted to follow the south-westerly course of the Kunene River, flying at low level just above the water. A few minutes later we observed a dust cloud, obviously caused by a vehicle travelling down the broad roadway along the eastern bank of the river. The roadway, running roughly north–south directly towards the border, consisted of a braid of countless paths cut through the deep riverine sand and thick bush by vehicles over many years and was, in places, up to 300 metres wide. Our curiosity immediately overtook caution and we manoeuvred the gunships into a position where we could 'peep' over the bank at the source of the dust cloud.

It turned out to be a tanker truck painted a uniform forest-green colour. Closer inspection revealed that there was only one occupant, the driver, who, despite wrestling fiercely with the steering wheel, was clearly having difficulty with the directional force imposed by the deep ruts in the sand. Upon leaving Vila

Roçadas he had probably hoped to set the hand throttle for a constant speed, let out the clutch to get the vehicle moving, remove his hands and feet from the controls and curl up for a nap until he reached his destination 60 kilometres away at Calueque. Fifty kilometres later, he was trying manfully to exercise some degree of control over the bucking tanker, but to no avail.

Some movement or sound must have got his attention. His head snapped to the right and he saw our two gunships, less than 100 metres way. Without hesitating for even a second, the driver opened the door and hurled himself out into space. He had barely touched the ground in a puff of dust before he shot off into the bush faster than my eyes could follow.

The tanker lumbered on down the road.

Unable to resist the temptation, our two gunships pulled back to a range of around 200 metres from the vehicle and I instructed my engineer to open fire with the 20 mm side-firing cannon, mounted where the Alo III's port sliding door would normally be.

The Oerlikon or Hispano 20 mm cannons mounted in our aircraft could fire 600 rounds of thumb-sized projectiles per minute, but good flight engineers would only fire two- to three-round bursts. Longer bursts affected the pilot's ability to control the aircraft, as the cannons had a fierce recoil, and the Alo III had really not been designed as a gunship.

The 250 rounds of ammunition for the gun were packed in an ammo pan fixed to the floor in the front of the aircraft and belt-fed to the gun's firing mechanism. (Later, the ammo pan was moved out of the cockpit and into the left rear luggage compartment.) Engineers normally loaded the ammo in the ratio of three solid or ball rounds to one high-explosive (HE) round. The HE rounds were, in effect, high-velocity fragmentation grenades.

Simultaneous two-to-three-shot bursts from the two gunships hit the tanker. Fluid emerged, staining the areas around the holes where the projectiles had penetrated.

'Hit it again,' I said, and my engineer squeezed the trigger again.

Whatever was in that tank I do not know, but there was a blinding flash as the contents exploded. The inspection hatch on the top of the 30 000-litre tank parted company from the main body and disappeared, hundreds of metres into the sky.

Instantaneously, the path that the hatch cover followed was tracked by an eye-scorchingly bright pale-blue column of flame that just climbed higher and higher and higher. It was still burning with high intensity about ten minutes later when I looked back on the scene while we streaked away (high speed is possible in an Alo III during those shit-yourself episodes), like bandits departing a bank robbery.

To be honest, we headed westwards in a naive attempt to avoid being linked to the destruction of the tanker, which, we figured, was unlikely to have been an authorised target or to have contributed much to the war effort. By giving Calueque and surrounds a wide berth, and approaching Ruacana from the direction of the Kaokoveld, to the west, we reckoned that if blame were to be apportioned, it would not be to us.

Very low on fuel, thanks to the detour we'd taken, we landed at Ruacana airfield about 45 minutes later. We observed that the entire staff complement of the base, and many of the townsfolk, had gathered at every elevated point, many with binoculars, all looking northwards, across the border and into Angola, where a thick column of smoke still spiralled tellingly into the sky.

'What are you looking at?' we asked, nonchalantly.

'There was an almighty explosion about an hour ago over there where that smoke stack is,' said a young officer pointing at the distant object. 'Didn't you guys see it from the air? It lit everything up!'

'Nah, we were at low level out there,' we said, probably too quickly, pointing vaguely to the distant Kaokoland mountains.

Chuffed with our brilliant ingenuity and spur-of-the-moment innovation under great pressure, we thought we'd escape unscathed, and the four of us agreed to keep the details of the incident under our bush hats. So, imagine our surprise when, at the next intelligence briefing, the intelligence officer turned to us and congratulated us on a job well done.

It seems that our actions in spontaneously taking out the tanker had significantly curtailed FAPLA activity in the Calueque area (we weren't told what mysterious substance the tanker was carrying), even though the attack was a violation of Angolan sovereignty, according to the United Nations, as officially we were not at war with Angola.

'How did you know it was us who *klapped* (hit) the truck?' we asked.

'Intelligence!' replied the officer proudly.

*

I got back home to Pretoria in early April and, for the first time since joining 17 Squadron, settled in, albeit briefly, to life as a squadron pilot. I caught up on training, doing short trips around the Pretoria area for any number of reasons, and also doing the odd one-to-four-night stop away from base.

Being at home base also allowed me to catch up with the social life I'd missed, for a number of months, enjoying drinks with friends in Pretoria's many fine pubs, catching the latest movies, attending live theatre and generally reconnecting with 'normal' life. I even managed to establish an exclusive relationship with a very fine lady called Desiree, who, less than a year later, would become my wife.

I had never been keen on, or comfortable with, the idea of living in the officers' mess, so I opted to rent a cottage in the garden of a Queen Street home, in the leafy Pretoria suburb of Irene, from a wonderfully kind widow, Mrs Merle Bradley. She flatly refused to take any rent from me while I was away 'doing your thing for the country', as she put it. She was also wise beyond words, and our late-night conversations around her kitchen table (she was an insomniac), after I'd returned from my nocturnal activities, arguably offered real solutions to more global problems than the United Nations General Assembly ever could.

*

One day in April 1980 I was sitting in the crew room at 17 Squadron when the ops clerk walked in and handed me a tasking signal with instructions from SAAF HQ to take an Alo III to Schmidtsdrift Weapons Testing Range that coming Sunday. For the duration of the following week, I was supposed to provide air support to a team of Armscor (the state-owned arms manufacturing company) and army boffins testing a new weapons system there.

Thinking that I had a rare weekend off, I had already made arrangements to have Sunday lunch with my parents and grand-mother on the family farm, ostensibly to introduce them to Desiree. By tradition, Joubert family lunches at the farm were noteworthy culinary events and were difficult to turn down.

Close scrutiny of the tasking signal offered a possible solution. I saw that I was only expected to be in Schmidtsdrift, which is about 90 kilometres west of Kimberley, by sundown on Sunday, in order to start work on the project first thing on Monday morning. I calculated that if an early meal at the farm could be arranged and I got airborne from AFB Swartkop by 14h30, I could still make it to Schmidtsdrift, on time, by sunset on Sunday evening.

My mom and dad had gone through a rough few years in the period prior to that April lunch, being torn hither and thither by a whole host of conflicts. Even though they had both tried to hide the friction from me, I was not the only one, as shallow as my sensitivity meter was set, to fear that they might even split up. But when I arrived at the farm that day, I sensed a whole new atmosphere. I realised quickly that, being the astounding and irrepressibly resilient couple that they were, and having overcome so much hardship between them, they had found each other again. I was overjoyed and watched their exchange of intimate looks with a sense of great delight.

The meal, attended by just the five of us – Mom, Dad, Gran, Desiree and me – was filled with joyous banter, laughter and warmth. At 13h30 I reluctantly excused myself and dashed for the airport.

I landed at Schmidtsdrift after a relatively uneventful three-hour flight and walked straight into a shitstorm. It seems that wires had somehow been crossed between the weapons project leader at Schmidtsdrift, an army brigadier and SAAF HQ, and that my presence had been required a lot earlier that Sunday.

The brigadier met me as I got out of my seat in the Alo.

'The fact that you have only just arrived,' the fellow (clearly a few sheets to the wind) informed me, while prodding his finger into my chest, 'has unduly delayed the project and I'll be taking punitive action against you, you fucking blue-job bicycle.'

After such a wonderful day, I really wasn't in the mood to be dictated to by a person under the influence, no matter what his rank, but I still bit down hard on my lip and said, with as much restraint as I could muster, 'Brigadier, here's the tasking signal that I got. If you read it you will see that it requires me to be here by this evening. If you don't like what it orders me to do, please take it up with SAAF HQ,' and I turned smartly away to help the flight engineer put the Alo to bed.

The brigadier threw the blue folder containing the tasking signal to the ground, and mumbling a string of profanities, interspersed with 'fucking' and 'bicycle', stormed off to wherever pissed-off brigs go in Schmidtsdrift.

During dinner that evening I was asked/told to attend a briefing immediately afterwards with the full team of big-bang and destruction-device experts. The brigadier opened the meeting with another assault on my alleged tardiness but was quickly silenced by one of the Armscor scientists, who then took charge and outlined the programme for the coming week. The combined team's requirement for chopper support was a lot more involved than I'd thought, and I looked forward to a busy week, despite the hostile attitude of the brig.

The meeting went on until around 22h30, and had just finished when a young national serviceman came into the room and made straight for me.

'Lieutenant Joubert?" he inquired.

'One and the same,' I responded.

'There's a phone call from Air Force Headquarters for you in the ops room, sir.'

'Are you sure it's for me?' I asked, surprised.

'Yes, sir. Please follow me,' and he led the way to a darkened tent where a landline had been tenuously connected to the primitive local telephone exchange network. As we walked the hundred or so metres to the ops room I felt an increasing sense of trepidation. Receiving a call in a place as remote as Schmidts-drift was rare, and I knew instinctively that it could only mean bad news.

I suspected that the brigadier had already lodged a complaint about my insolence and that, at the least, the call was going to be an unmitigated dressing-down from some ranking desk pilot at SAAF HQ.

'Lieutenant Joubert,' I said hesitantly, after picking up the phone transceiver.

'Lieutenant,' said a voice on the other end of the line, 'this is the duty officer at SAAF HQ. I have some bad news for you—' and then the line went dead.

By now I was convinced that the brigadier had shopped me to SAAF HQ for something I'd not done, and I was plotting my revenge when the phone rang again. I picked it up.

'Hello, Lieutenant. This line is … mother's had a … intensive care … get back to Pretoria asap. Your replacement … be there tomorrow … 10h00.'

The call dropped for the second time, and, despite the young national serviceman doing all in his power and winding the handle until it glowed red hot, we couldn't re-establish contact with SAAF HQ.

For the first time in my life I felt a sense of dread so deep and so strong that I battled to breathe. I concentrated hard to calm myself but couldn't suppress the blind panic that I felt welling up in my chest. I tried to convince myself that it couldn't be true, that someone had made a monumental error and confused me with some other Joubert, but deep down I knew that something terrible had happened to my mother.

Going back over the call, I came to the conclusion that Mom had in all likelihood been hurt in a car accident. But then, what of Dad, who would have been with her, or my gran, who they would have been taking home? There'd been no mention of them. At some point, I realised that the sooner I left for home, the better.

It was not a good idea, and a prohibited practice, to fly an Alo III at night without any visible moon and as my poor luck would have it, there was no moon that night. I went in search of the brigadier to inform him of my imminent departure and to apologise for the inconvenience that this would cause. I found him in the ablution block brushing his teeth and preparing for bed.

'Brigadier, I just got a call from SAAF HQ. Something very serious has happened to my mother and I am leaving for Pretoria as soon as conditions allow. My replacement will be here at 10h00 tomorrow, I think.'

'Fuck,' he said, spraying flecks of toothpaste and spit onto the mirror in front of him. 'You fucking blue-jobs and your never-ending namby-pamby excuses will have consequences. You should realise, my boy, that when you are a soldier you must put the bullshit of families behind the needs of your country!'

'You don't know my mom,' I said, and walked swiftly away, afraid that I'd do or say something that I'd later regret.

Sleep was impossible, and I tossed and turned until around 03h30 or so, when I woke my flight engineer and said I was leaving, in the dark with no moon. If he wanted to stay put I'd understand, but I needed to get to Pretoria. True to the character of SAAF flight engineers, he reached the chopper before I did and we left shortly afterwards. I was fortunate that the sky was clear and that a dull line on the horizon allowed me to keep the aircraft the right way up and to avoid trouble.

After a brief vertical descent and landing in the courtyard of the police station at Wolmaransstad to refuel, we took off into a lightening eastern sky and landed at AFB Swartkop just before 07h00. On the final leg, I had managed to contact a radio ham, and the extraordinarily helpful operator kindly patched my radio call into a telephone and called my sister, who also lived in Pretoria. She then gave me the gist of what had transpired.

Our mom had suffered a stroke.

The previous evening, as she and my dad were driving my grandmother back into Pretoria, without any warning Mom had collapsed in the front passenger seat of the car. They were close to the Pretoria General Hospital and my dad had driven straight to the casualty section. Consequently, Mom had received treatment within minutes for the blood clot lodging in her brain.

For now, that was all she knew. I told my sister that I'd be at the hospital around 07h30.

I don't think that the rotor blades of the Alo had even stopped before I leapt out and rushed off to my car. Peak-hour traffic notwithstanding, I reached the hospital 20 minutes later and sprinted all the way to the ward where my dad and sister were waiting.

All night long, tossing and turning in my bed at Schmidtsdrift and during the flight home, I had tried to picture what I'd see when I finally got to my mother's bedside. At the tender age of 21, I had become accustomed to, and had no great fear or dread of seeing blood and guts, severed body parts or gaping violent injuries to the bodies of human beings. I rationalised that they were part and parcel of the work I'd chosen to do, and the price I needed to pay for a career in the aviation industry.

I thought, irrationally, that this was the worst I was likely to encounter when I got to Mom's bedside. But nothing and no one could have prepared me for what I saw. I was only vaguely aware of the presence of other people, and all I heard was the subdued hum of machines. Sunlight streamed in through a window.

Mom was lying on her back under clean white sheets and a hospital blanket was drawn up to her neck, with just her head, shoulders and arms visible. There was a drip inserted into her right hand and someone was holding her left, which they relinquished to me. Her hand was clammy and cool, if not cold, to the touch.

For some reason, the first thing that profoundly disturbed me was the sight of two transparent plastic pipes running from under the sheets and into her nose. Then I saw that her lips were slightly parted and that the plastic tube from a ventilator leading into her mouth was distorting the left side of her face. I could also hear a faint bubbling sound, but I couldn't work out where it was coming from.

But the thing that shattered any hope I may have harboured for her return to vitality was Mom's half-opened eyes.

They gave forth nothing.

They were glazed and blank, and I knew then that her soul was already elsewhere. Slowly, like being pulled into a dark cave, the dullness in those eyes began to draw me in until it held my complete attention.

I stood there, unable to resist being consumed by the nameless thing that had invaded the shell of the exquisitely beautiful woman who'd given me life, who'd always known instinctively when I needed her and into whose loving embrace I'd been so utterly sure I could escape whenever things got too tough.

I found myself fighting a black, looming wave that grew so rapidly that it blocked out everything and everyone in the room. I felt myself struggling not to scream, to rant, to rage. I wanted to thrash the doctors who'd failed to fix her when she'd needed them most, and to rail at my dad, who couldn't stop this cowardly faceless thing from stealing her from me.

I wanted to obliterate anyone I could blame for causing the agony that was tearing me apart.

At the height of my fury, I found myself suddenly standing a short distance away, observing the unfolding scene. Then, in a moment of great light and clarity, it suddenly struck me that my furious need to hold the whole world culpable for this terrible, terrible loss should rather be directed inwards.

I wasn't ready to do that.

So I turned and ran away.

*

In the days that followed, surgeons told the family that the stroke had impacted the motor centre of Mom's brain, and that her prognosis was extremely poor. There was no hope of her ever again regaining consciousness. She would be comatose for the rest of her days.

I found it difficult to visit when other people were with her, and so I started going alone and late at night. I'd hold her hand and talk to her, hoping against hope that she was listening. I'd stare intently into her eyes or just wish vainly for some flicker of reaction, some recognition, some sign of life.

But there was none.

At just after 05h00 on the fourth day after our world had stopped turning, I woke up after another restless night. I immediately became aware of a sense of foreboding

Mildly perturbed, I nevertheless decided to start the day a little earlier than normal. I showered, shaved and dressed before making a cup of coffee and sitting down at the little desk that served as my dining table.

At just before 06h00 I heard Desiree's car pull into the driveway.

I heard her get out and the car door close.

Then I heard a subdued conversation between her and Mrs Bradley, who'd gone out to meet her.

I heard them walk up to my front door and rap softly.

I opened the door. Both women stood there, tears coursing down their cheeks.

At 05h15 that Thursday morning the embolism had moved into Mom's brain and doused the last flickering vestiges of her life.

She was only 45.

*

Throughout those indescribably sad days that followed, first notifying friends and family, then making the funeral arrangements, and finally the awful bruising trauma of Mom's cremation service at the Rebecca Street Chapel, the emotional paralysis in me held firm. It allowed me to function, albeit like an automaton.

I have no detailed memories of that time other than of the tsunami of shock and grief that drenched everyone. The depth of sadness at her passing stunned friends, family and associates. It was born of her unbridled joy for life, of her smile, which could soften even the hardest of hearts, and of her selflessness, which noticeably affected everyone she ever encountered.

I was around 16 when I'd found a diary entry that she'd written on her 16th birthday, the day she had rebelled against the selfish summons of her own mother to leave school to come back to Brakpan and work. I cannot recall the exact wording, but I do recall her making a promise to herself to the effect that 'I will never treat my own children like this, NEVER. I will love and support them with all my heart so that they never have to experience the feelings of pain, rejection and sorrow that I feel right now.'

She was unwavering in living out that promise, to the day she died.

As her funeral ended, the minister who'd performed the service approached our family – my dad, my gran, my brother, my sister and me. He offered words of comfort to each of us in turn. As he did so, I watched myself go through the motions of a grieving son, from a short distance away, just like I did when things got hairy in the bush.

I remember thinking that I should be crying, but, frustratingly, I couldn't find the button that would open the floodgates to my

My mom, Inez Ursula Joubert (née Wilson), 18 July 1934 – 24 April 1980

tears. When the minister reached me, he looked into my dry eyes, leant forward and embraced me. As he did so he whispered, 'Let go, Stephen. Just let go. You must not hold back the feelings inside. If you do so, you will hurt yourself and all of those around you. Let go, Stephen. Please let go.'

'I'm fine,' I said.

Ten years later, I was still occasionally picking up the phone to call my mom.

8

Escalation and intensification

In the weeks and months that followed, I did the only logical thing that I knew and buried myself in my work, spending more time in the bush than I did at home.

At Ondangwa, I'd make sure that I was in the vanguard of helicopter operations and thus spent considerable time away from the relative comforts of the base, at one stage even spending a few nights in a hole dug into the barren soil somewhere in southern Angola.

My recall of events during this time is not very sharp and some notable incidents are lumped together in my memory, adversely affecting chronological accuracy. However, I do remember that in June 1980, I went to Windhoek for a short tour of two weeks. I had barely unpacked my bags when a call came through for me to pack a small overnight bag and wait to be taken to Eros airport to catch a flight to an undisclosed destination.

On arrival at the airport, my flight engineer, Douw Kuhn, and I were bundled aboard a Beechcraft Queen Air and flown to AFB Ondangwa, which I'd left two weeks previously. When we arrived there later that night, I was told that an Alo III gunship had been shot down that afternoon about 70 kilometres inside Angola, and that the crew were missing and presumed killed. The flight engineer and I were to replace them on the operation that was already well under way.

The crew of the ill-fated Alo gunship, Captain Thinus van Rensburg and flight engineer Sergeant Koos Cilliers, were colleagues from 17 Squadron at AFB Swartkop. Koos lost his life in the incident, while Thinus, despite fracturing his spine, managed to evade capture and walked about 30 kilometres to safety during that night, presenting himself to South African forces entrenched near Cuamato, in southern Angola, the following morning.

The suggestion that I pack an overnight bag was somewhat optimistic, and it was a full seven to ten days later that the operation ended. The chopper crews returned to Ondangwa, and Douw and I were urged to try to scrounge a lift on any transport aircraft going in the direction of Windhoek. Rather than wait for a 'commando' (civilian volunteer) aircraft to be organised to get us back to Windhoek, Douw and I, still in our fragrant 'overnight' flying overalls, managed to hitch a ride on a 44 Squadron Dakota going that way.

The skipper of the Dak, Trevor Watkins, had been doing a tour of the operational area with a bunch of States-based schoolteachers, all male, as part of the SADF's border awareness programme. In theory, the teachers were looking over various bases, courtesy of the South African taxpayer, to see the conditions prevailing for the soldiers stationed there. The idea was that they would return to their schools in the new term better informed and able to dispel some of the untruths, fears and legends about military life for schoolboys entering national service in the following year.

The Dak's engines had already been started when Douw and I clambered aboard the aircraft. We could see that it was full, not just because the 20 or so teachers were occupying every available seat along either side of the fuselage, but also because there was an enormous pile of beer secured under a cargo net in the middle of the floor.

With a paucity of space available to plant our backsides, Douw and I retired to the very rear of the aircraft and sat on the floor near the rear door.

We got airborne at about 15h00 for the three-hour flight. The outside air temperature was at least 38°C. It was even hotter inside the aircraft.

It quickly became apparent that the teachers had imbibed copious amounts of the amber nectar prior to take-off. However, the quaffing of the brewer's best quickly tapered off once we were in the air, due to the extreme turbulence as the Dak flew at low level to avoid the threat of missiles.

We stopped briefly at Grootfontein to drop off some urgent correspondence and took off again into the late afternoon heat haze and unceasing turbulence. Although the crew tried manfully to climb above it, their efforts were to no avail.

The interior of an airborne Dakota is not a quiet place. Douw and I sat in the back, minding our own business, dozing a little and enjoying the odd bit of amber nectar ourselves. At one point, I looked up at the educators and noticed that, to a man, they were all sweating profusely. Their colour had changed dramatically, and some of them were swallowing faster than a wild dog at an impala kill.

I had recently read Pat Conroy's *The Great Santini*, a book about US Marine pilots and their antics around the world in the 1960s. Drawing directly on an anecdote in the book, and to relieve the boredom of the flight, a plan formed in my head and I quietly briefed Douw.

First, I concealed an opened bottle of Colt 45 lager in the breast pocket of my flying overall. Then I got to my feet and staggered through the passenger cabin towards the forward bulkhead where the barf bags were stowed in stacks, held in place by two leather straps. These receptacles were in full view of all needy passengers. Along the way, I kept apologising to the wide-eyed teachers, while gulping furiously and saying, 'Sorry chaps, but ... I fly every ... day and I ... am feeling ... very, very ill right now. I don't know .... how you ... are keeping it in!'

Then I dashed to the barf bag holder, frantically grabbed one of the semi-opaque plastic packets and stuck my upper body into the passageway leading to the cockpit so that the teachers couldn't see my face. All they could make out in the fading light was my back and shoulders and my heaving spasmodically and theatrically at regular intervals as I pretended to vomit, loudly and continuously, into the barf bag.

While carrying on this gut-churning pretence, I slipped the bottle of beer out of my pocket and poured the contents into the barf bag, hiding the empty bottle under the navigator's table when the bag was sufficiently full. Then I turned around and lurched towards the rear of the aircraft carrying the bag, with the partially visible contents frothing and sloshing around for everyone to see.

The shell-shocked teachers were stunned motionless by the spectacle of an SAAF pilot, a frequent flyer, a man who made his living in the air, carrying a bag of vomit. Just when the shock and horror were reaching fever pitch, Douw shouted from the back of the cabin with all the contempt he could muster, 'Bliksem, Loot, you can't waste good beer like that!' He then ran up to me, snatched the bag like it was a prized family possession ... and emptied the contents into his mouth.

For a second there was silence, with only the drone of the Dak's engines at cruising speed burbling in the background. Then there erupted a scene of such violent gastric voiding, accompanied by such primal screeching, that any observer entering the cabin at that point would have been excused for thinking they had arrived in the dungeons of hell itself. Cheeks puffed up like footballs as the teachers fought desperately to contain the explosions erupting from their guts. Momentarily, time and motion seemed to slow right down, but then a thin stream of variously coloured soup-like liquid spewed from the corner of one man's tightly pursed lips and arced clear across the cabin to splatter against the inside of one of the Dak's square windows, narrowly missing the ear of the bespectacled gentleman sitting opposite him. Every available container that could be used as a receptacle – bush hats, canvas kit bags, padded camera boxes and even a very large sombrero – was grasped with gusto. One chap employed the hollowed-out cavity in a large upturned Ovambo drum belonging to the fellow sitting next to him.

To a man, the teachers threw what my dad later referred to as 'multiple, insistent, hydraulic yodels', until none of them had the strength to expel any more material. Blobs of muck merged with squirting perspiration and stained the collars of their 'I was there!' T-shirts.

I know not who cleaned the aircraft when we got to Windhoek an hour or so later. I do know, however, that Douw and I, fearing for our personal safety, slipped away in a great hurry as soon as the cargo door opened at Eros airport. I am aware that there is a strong likelihood that our actions did not endear us to the contingent of educators on that fateful flight, and I would like to take this opportunity to tender my sincere apologies to them.

*

I was back in Ondangs a month or so later.

During this time Richie Verschoor, in another gunship, and I had gone out to Nkongo to assist the army with a local sweep. It ended too late for us to return to Ondangs, so we decided to bed down at Nkongo for the night. It turned out to be a sleepless night, because the Nkongo base protection detail fellows blasted away at regular intervals with a battery of light and heavy machine guns at distant 'attackers' who, they told us, could be seen moving between the trees about 500 metres away.

Their quick response, they said, was preventing the execution of a PLAN mortar assault, no doubt aimed at the two Alo III gunships tucked away behind the base's five-metre-high revetments. The prompt action of the army units based at Nkongo no doubt saved the day (or night), as the 'substantial force of assailants' was unable to fire even a single mortar or rifle round in our direction. However, when a well-equipped patrol was dispatched in the cold light of the following morning to sweep through the area where the PLAN fighters had apparently been seen, only the remains of a drove of 12 or so dead donkeys could be found.

Thanking our lucky stars that the donkeys had been unable to breach Nkongo's formidable defences, Richie Verschoor and I headed 170 kilometres west to Ombalantu to join the main force of a new operation starting from there the following day.

When we arrived at Ombalantu to attend the pre-ops briefing, we were told that there was a shortage of accommodation at the base itself, but that accommodation had been arranged for us at a nearby base called Ogongo, located on the main Oshakati–Ruacana road. After the briefing, we took off into the fading light of the evening sky and landed in near darkness at Ogongo base a short while later.

A chap in civilian clothes met us as we landed. Once we'd settled the two aircraft down for the night, making sure they would be safe from being damaged by local livestock, he led the four of us (our engineers included) to a tent with four beds in it. We deposited our overnight bags in the tent and our guide offered to show us to the mess and pub, not necessarily in that order.

I remember finding it slightly odd that all the Ogongo base personnel were dressed in civilian clothes but thought nothing more about it.

Upon entering the pub, I sought out and introduced myself and Richie to the senior rank, whom everyone else referred to as 'the Major'. Much later, when the pub eventually closed, the Major extended an invitation to the four aircrew to join him in his operations room, where a large stash of liquor resided and where the consumption of alcohol would continue. Obviously, unwilling to offend our host, we complied and soon found ourselves in a large tent containing a couple of fridges filled with soft and hard drinks.

We were joined there by the remaining patrons of the pub. Things got quite raucous, with us leading the singing of ribald rugby songs that reverberated through the camp. A while later I noticed that Richie, notorious throughout southern Africa for his misbehaviour after consuming even small quantities of fermented beverages, was having a spirited conversation with one of the other patrons. Then he suddenly stepped back and roared at the top of his lungs, drowning out all the other sounds of revelry, 'I HATE THE FUCKING SAP! SHOW ME A COP RII-IGHT NOW AND I'LL KICK HIS FUCKING ARSE!'

Just seconds later, as if they'd been waiting in the shadows for just this eventuality, a string of five or six strapping youngsters filed into the ops tent armed with standard-issue *balsakke* (canvas kitbags) the contents of which were likely to affect the bodily health of anyone caught in their path if they happened to be violently swung as a weapon in a fight, which suddenly seemed imminent.

But between who and who, I asked myself.

'The SAAF versus you fuzz motherfuckers!' Richie roared ... and I realised suddenly, to my great dismay, that he was referring to himself, me and our two engineers on the one side, and the rest of the base on the other.

'Where are you off to, you fucking cowards?' Richie shouted, not at the would-be assassins standing in front of us (as I would have preferred) but at our two engineers. Knowing hopeless odds when they saw them, the two had made a beeline for a gap between the tent's roof and its walls and were making good their escape through the hole and into the darkness beyond.

'It looks like it's just you and me, Stevie my boy! Let's give these slopeheads the hiding of their lives!' Richie roared, with a lot more confidence than I would ever have mustered when facing certain death.

'There are 600 of my SAP *manne* (men) in this camp,' interceded the Major calmly, stepping between the warring factions with his hands held up, like a pointsman directing traffic at a major intersection. 'Are you sure that you want to beat them all up tonight?' he asked, the question directed more at me than at Richie, probably because he could see my knees knocking and had noticed the absence of any visible scarring on my youthful face, a sure indicator that I was unaccustomed to having the shit kicked out of me.

'We will have to discuss it between the two of us,' I said firmly, hoping to retain some dignity.

I shuffled Richie, holding one hand over his mouth to avoid any further incitement of violence, through a hissing gauntlet of angry South African policemen just itching to add our scalps to their unit totem pole.

'Be patient,' I whispered softly to him. 'Revenge is sweet.'

We retired to our beds without further incident.

At 04h30, our engineers woke us and we made our way to the two helicopters. After a thorough preflight inspection, we started the engines and prepared for flight.

As I lifted my chopper into the air I told Richie over the radio, 'Follow me', and we air-taxied, ten or so metres off the ground, to and fro, over the SAP Ogongo camp, using the downwash from the rotor blades to drive great quantities of dust, dirt and plant matter, at very high speed, into every crevice and orifice of the tents and offending SAP members below.

Doesn't he who laughs last, laugh longest?

*

The run-in, at just above the tops of the trees, to the target that morning, a well-defended PLAN base about 90 kilometres inside Angola, for some reason or other remains vivid in my mind.

We'd flown in the pitch darkness from Ogongo to Ombalantu where we'd refuelled, gulped a quick cup of coffee and a 'dog biscuit' (a square, flavourless, chalky concoction of sawdust and low-grade flour) and donned flak jackets before taking off for the forthcoming battle, behind another six gunships who'd all spent the previous night at Ombalantu, offending no one in particular.

It was just starting to get light in the eastern sky as we crossed the cutline, proceeding roughly east-northeast towards the PLAN camp, which, our intelligence reports told us, contained 800 well-armed troops. We were also likely to encounter 14.5 mm anti-aircraft guns, as well as RPG-7s and SAM-7s, they said.

The flak jacket I wore was particularly uncomfortable and felt as heavy as a small car. In fact, the 'steel-plates-in-pockets' type of flak jacket, which we used long before today's ultra-lightweight Kevlar models, was a relic from the Second World War. They were individually 'constructed' by selecting armoured steel panels about ten centimetres square from a large pile provided and sliding them into any number of pockets sewn onto the jacket itself, ostensibly to protect the more vulnerable parts of your torso. I always overdid the number of panels and would invariably end up with blood blisters on my bum wherever the weight of the jacket merged with sweat and interfaced with cotton underwear, Nomex flying overall and canvas seat cover.

The flak jacket also severely restricted movement, and I generally discarded the ruddy thing at the first available opportunity. This usually happened after departing the battle scene for the helicopter administrative area (HAA), which was typically established some distance from the battle site to permit choppers to refuel and rearm and to allow the crews to grab a rare-grilled rump steak and chips (read: dog biscuit and battery acid) without drifting too far from the fight.

The approach to the target that morning took longer than usual, probably a full 30 minutes. This gave me the time to prepare mentally for the coming punch-up, which in my case simply meant three things: making myself as small a target as possible (not easy when you have three tons of metal plates in your shirt; trying (unsuccessfully) to forget that the wraparound Perspex windshield was only two millimetres thick; and considering (briefly) that most folks back home in the States were likely tucking into bacon and eggs or corn flakes at that very moment.

When the gunships were still around ten kilometres out, I could clearly see the Mirages and Impalas striking the target with bombs and rockets, and the anticipated response from the defenders lighting up the early morning sky like a misplaced fireworks display.

Although I had previously observed SAAF jets attacking a target and the response by the enemy's anti-aircraft weaponry, that morning's defensive reaction seemed a lot more intense than I'd seen before, and my trepidation increased. Eventually this caused my consciousness to become detached from my body and to locate itself ten or so metres away, so that I could observe myself going through the motions of flying the aircraft into the heat of the battle without concern for my well-being.

With two kilometres for us to go, the jets left the scene, the gunships climbed to their operating height of 200 to 300 metres and we spread out into a circle around the target area, ostensibly to take out any remaining resistance on the ground.

My initial impression was that the jets had done a good job. There were fires burning all over the target area, and sporadic explosions as exposed ordnance ignited. There appeared to be no enemy troops, however, which flew in the face of the anti-aircraft response we'd just witnessed, as well as that morning's last-minute update from our reconnaissance scouts, who at 05h00 had reported the presence of 800 PLAN soldiers.

We flew in circles for ten minutes or so without anything notable happening, and then the gunship formation leader, Neil Ellis, instructed us to form four separate two-ship 'orbits' to the north, east, south and west of the target camp and to focus our attention on clearing the designated landing zones of any potential threats. This was to prepare for the arrival of troop-carrying Puma helicopters, which were just minutes out from disgorging their human cargo.

Richie Verschoor and I took the southern orbit.

The western orbit was taken by Arthur Walker and his wingman, Peter Hanes, who had arrived for his first tour on Alos just a few days before. Arthur Walker had a penchant for occasionally drifting off to look for trouble. Unbeknown to any of us, he flew off to look at something that had caught his interest some distance away and left Peter to do the boring work of circling over a designated Puma LZ, a patch of grassland around 500 metres west of the main target area.

At that moment, there was quite a bit of radio chatter going on as we tried to work out why and how the enemy soldiers had managed to evacuate the target area so quickly. Neil Ellis polled the older, more experienced gunship commanders, asking each for his considered opinion of the state of play.

During a momentary break in the radio chatter Peter Hanes calmly said, 'Guys, I am drawing some fire from a 14.5 gun emplacement. Please would someone come and help me, as Arthur has gone off to play somewhere on his own?'

I remember thinking at that moment that Pete was obviously confusing the sparks from a burning truck with the lethal 14.5 mm trio of spitting death (a 14.5 emplacement was a battery of three 14.5 mm anti-aircraft guns, normally deployed in a triangle with the guns set around ten metres apart and each gun manned by a team of three). And, in any event, no one could be so calm and conversational while his backside was being shot at.

So, no one reacted to his request for help, although the radio chatter did briefly die down a bit. Thirty seconds or so passed and then Pete said, slightly more agitated but not so you'd become concerned at all, 'Guys, I have taken out all three 14.5 guns. Please, someone come across here and I can show you where they are.'

Still no response came from the other disbelieving gunship pilots.

Another 20 seconds passed.

Then, getting quite exasperated, Pete said, 'I have a yellow fuel-booster-pump caution light which has illuminated and I think that I must go to the HAA to check it out. Would someone please come across here so that I can show them where these buggers are?'

I was the closest, so I offered to go to where he was, but by the time I got there he was already at treetop level and heading for the HAA, so he quickly described the whereabouts of the guns to me on the VHF radio and left the scene. Following his directions, but still not really believing that they were of any great effect or substance, I looked down at the *shona* (grassy area) where the six Pumas were about to land ... and almost had a heart attack.

On the edge of the *shona*, with a perfect field of fire over the LZ, were three Russian-made 14.5 mm anti-aircraft guns deployed in the customary triangle. Spread around the anchor plates of each gun were their recently expired three-man crews. Closer inspection later revealed that the guns had all been disabled by extraordinarily accurate 20 mm cannon fire from Pete Hanes's gunship and carried out by his flight engineer, Flippie Rohm.

'Sheeeeeeeeitttt, guys,' I said over the radio, 'Pete wasn't joking. There really are three 14.5s and a bunch of dead fellows around them ... Come look see!'

A few minutes later Richie Verschoor and I left the target area to refuel at the HAA. While the engine of my gunship was shutting down, I looked across to my left where Pete Hanes's Alo was parked 20 or so metres away. The entire tail boom appeared to be wet and was shining brightly in the early morning sun.

I got out and strolled across to Pete's gunship. He was sitting on the ground just to the left of the aircraft, with Flippie Rohm next to him. They were both pale and staring intently at the Alo's 450-litre fuel tank through the open luggage compartment door at the left rear of the fuselage.

Closer inspection revealed why. In the process of 'taking out' the three 14.5 mm anti-aircraft guns, the gunship had been hit by two separate 14.5 mm rounds. The first had struck the base of the fuel tank and left a gaping hole in its wake before travelling up through the fuel and striking the float mechanism, which measures fuel contents, jamming it in the 'full' position.

The second round had impacted the steel plates, situated roughly halfway up the fuel tank on either side, into which the cable assembly that suspends the tank above the floor of the fuselage passes. The result was that the aircraft immediately started losing whatever fuel was left in the tank, but no 'low fuel' indication appeared in the cockpit as the float was jammed in the 'full' position.

Pete said that the rudders had initially become stiff and difficult to operate, but control had largely returned by the time he landed at the HAA. The stiffness was caused by the heavy fuel tank dropping down onto the rudder control cables that run along the bottom of the fuselage, but then, as the fuel gushed out, the tank had become lighter, which relieved the pressure and permitted relatively normal rudder control. Pete would have had no indication whatsoever of the impending engine failure when the fuel eventually ran out. This would have almost certainly occurred directly above the 'hot' battlefield.

What had saved his aircraft and crew was that, in the heat of the battle to eliminate the 14.5s, a PLAN soldier must have fired his AK-47 at the circling gunship and a round from the weapon had impacted the cigarette-box-sized fuel booster pump attached to the top of the Alo's turbine engine. This had caused a yellow caution light to illuminate in the cockpit. Even then, a yellow light is normally a warning that something inessential to the safe operation of the aircraft is failing or has failed and needs to be checked out at the next available opportunity. A red light, such as 'Fuel low', means that an essential component is failing and immediate action is required to prevent a catastrophe.

Pete's decision to act instantly on the yellow light had, in all probability, saved him, his engineer and the aircraft. I never established whether he got due credit for his actions.

*

Back at 17 Squadron in Pretoria a few weeks later, I was ordered to serve out an ED (extra duty, a favourite form of punishment for young SAAF officers) for some earlier indiscretions, the causes of which I cannot recall. Extra duty was quite a frequent occurrence during my Air Force career, and was occasioned typically by such mortal sins as wearing my flying jacket outside the confines of the base or having hair a little longer than regulations required. On this occasion, I was required to be the AFB Swartkop orderly officer between 18h00 and 06h00. This was tantamount to a base night manager. It was a function with which I had become quite familiar as I tried, ever in vain, to reduce the number of EDs that I still had to serve to a manageable quantity.

The orderly officer was required to sleep in a designated room on the base on the nights that he pulled duty. So, when 17 Squadron's operations clerk walked into the crew room, just as I was preparing to depart for the orderly officer's digs to while away the dark hours, and asked whether I'd be interested in doing a trip the next day, I accepted.

The envisaged flight entailed taking an Alo III from 17 Squadron early the next morning, collecting an army general (one General Hanekom) and his aide from the Movements Control area at Swartkop at 06h00, and flying them to the army base at Amsterdam, near the border with Swaziland, to attend a parade. We would return to AFB Swartkop later the same afternoon.

By the standards of the day, this was a simple two-leg mission – there and back in one day. Total flying time would be about four and a half hours. I had never been to Amsterdam, Transvaal, before, so I looked forward to the trip. I also figured that I could relieve some of the boredom of the ED by doing all my route preparation in the orderly officer's room that evening.

As I was leaving the squadron that evening, the operations clerk ran out and told me that notification had just come through that the mission take-off time had been moved to 07h00 the next morning and not 06h00, as originally stated on the tasking signal. But, being in a hurry, I didn't wait for the written confirmation of the later take-off time.

I checked in to the orderly officer's post just before 18h00, had something to eat and then returned to the squadron planning room to continue with the route preparation, which I completed by 22h00. This included a series of calls to the meteorological office at AFB Waterkloof to confirm weather conditions along the route for the next morning.

'Weather will be a bit kak early on, Lieutenant,' warned the meteorologist. 'Low cloud and mist all the way to Ermelo, but the worst is that the maximum air temperature will vary between only minus five and plus three degrees Celsius.'

'Colder than a witch's heart,' I chuckled. 'I'll dress warmly and I hope my passengers do too.'

The following morning when I woke at 05h00, I called the met office again. There was no real improvement in the weather and confirmation that the mist and low cloud would probably start to lift after 07h00. As far as the temperature was concerned, brass monkeys were advised to cover their groins with additional layers of warm clothing.

I dressed very snugly indeed, with three or four layers of thermal clothing to insulate me. Looking a bit like the Oros man I made my way to 17 Squadron, where the designated Alo awaited. During the preflight inspection, my flight engineer for the day, Johnny Smith, and I picked up a problem that needed to be fixed before we could fly. As the repair was unlikely to take too long, it would not delay the scheduled 07h00 take-off unduly. I was not perturbed and told Johnny to take his time. The longer we stayed on the ground, the more likely it was for the clouds and mist to lift and allow us safe passage, particularly across the elevated sections of the eastern Highveld.

I phoned the Movements Control office and told the chap who answered to please look out for an army general and inform him that there might be a small delay in wheels-up time but that it was not expected to be significant.

'Make him a nice cup of hot beverage and we'll be there in a jiffy,' I said brightly.

At around 07h00, Johnny walked in and told me that the aircraft was repaired and that we could go when ready. I walked out into the frigid air, conducted a full preflight check on the chopper again, started up and air-taxied down to Movements Control to collect my passengers. As the Alo settled onto the concrete slab in front of the entrance to the Movements Control area VIP lounge, I initiated the engine shutdown. Just then, movement at the edge of my peripheral vision caused me to turn my head 90 degrees to the left, where I observed a strange sight.

Emerging from a long black Mercedes-Benz was a clearly agitated senior army officer, possibly a general, with another army officer, a colonel, trying to placate him. The general was gesticulating wildly, with lots of clenched fists and a flurry of punches being thrown at an imaginary opponent.

'I wonder what's got up that pongo's nose?' I asked myself, as the chopper's rotor blades slowed and began to droop against their stops.

Convinced that his odd behaviour had nothing to do with me, I focused on watching the Alo's rotor and engine RPM indicators wind down. Suddenly I became aware of someone running towards the port side of the aircraft – a dangerous thing to do when the rotors are slowing. Looking up, I could see that the irate general had broken free of his colleague and was making his way at great speed towards my aircraft.

Fearing that he would be decapitated by the whirling rotor blades, I thrust out my gloved left hand aggressively at his advancing figure in the universal gesture to halt. My prompt action, which probably saved the unappreciative officer's life, formed the basis for the first of 14 counts under the Military Discipline Code (MDC) that he would later charge me with, namely, 'Insubordination, count 1'.

As soon as the blades had stopped spinning, he charged into the aircraft and began to curse me for my tardiness. From the way he was ranting and raving, I don't think that the boys in blue were his favourite arm of the service. He had almost certainly experienced a delay or two at the hands of some of my less time-aware colleagues in the SAAF.

However, I was not late and I told him so.

'I had arranged for a 06h00 take-off and it's already past 07h00!' he shouted.

Thus, the first count of Absent Without Leave was born and the tally of charges rose to two.

'Well, General, I was told that the take-off time was 07h00,' I said, perhaps not as subserviently as I could have (but then again he was shouting at me), 'and it's 07h00 now. Also, I asked the Movements Control personnel to advise you that we may be a little late and to take care of you, but it seems that you did not avail yourself of the Movements Control facilities?'

This statement resulted in 'Insubordination, count 2'.

'Get this chopper into the air now and make sure I am in Amsterdam on time!' he demanded.

'I must first complete the paperwork at Movements before we can leave, General,' I said, and strolled off into the building while he was still shouting. This resulted in 'Insubordination, count 3' and 'Disobeying a Lawful Command, count 1'.

The charge tally was now up to five, and we hadn't even left the ground.

After completing the relevant paperwork in record time, I got back into the Alo and started up but realised quickly that I couldn't hear the radio chatter because the general was still bellowing at me into the microphone of his headset at full volume. So, I disconnected him by (not completely) pulling out his headset plug. This resulted in 'Insubordination, count 4'.

Eventually the general stopped spitting and spluttering and we proceeded on our way, but goodness me, was it freezing. Johnny and I were okay because we'd dressed for the occasion, but the general and his aide had only pongo step-outs on and they were freezing!

'Put the heater on!' came the order from behind.

Now, anyone who flew Alos at 17 Squadron will know that the heater controls in the cockpits of our choppers were not connected to the hot-air bleed on the engines, as they were in Bloemfontein, for instance, as this adversely affected the total power output of the engines (or so I was told). It was no use switching them to the 'on' position as they simply wouldn't feed hot air into a freezing-cold passenger cabin.

'I am so sorry, General,' I replied (with just a touch of smugness), 'this aircraft doesn't have a heater.'

With the wisdom of hindsight, perhaps I should have said that the heater 'wasn't connected', as the 'heater' control lever, located in a control panel in the centre of the Alo III's roof, was in full view of the general.

'I said switch it on! I am freezing to death!'

'It won't work.'

'Switch the fucking thing on!'

So, I obliged him, knowing full well that it would not make an iota of difference to the polar conditions prevailing in the cabin, but I was striving desperately to establish a toehold of cordiality and to keep what little peace there was left among the occupants of my aircraft. The cockpit immediately started to heat up.

Alo 513 just happened to be the only Alo III at 17 Squadron with the heater control connected to the hot air bleed on the engine. 'Disobeying a Lawful Command, count 2' and 'Malicious Damage to State Property, count 1' stemmed from this altercation.

The charge score moved up to eight.

About two hours after leaving Pretoria, we landed at the army base at Amsterdam. Without a word to me, the fuming but warmer general stormed off with the base commanding officer to attend to whatever visiting brass do before important parades.

At lunch in the pongo officers' mess, I suggested to the general's aide, the colonel, that because the general parade was being held at the local rugby stadium and not at the base (I had been told that the crowd would number in the thousands, far too many to be accommodated at the base itself), perhaps I should collect the general from the rugby stadium and prevent any further wasting of time by waiting for him to return to the base.

Agreeing with me that this seemed like a fine fence-mending idea, the aide chatted to the general, who agreed wholeheartedly. I overheard him say to the colonel, 'That is the first decent suggestion that the blue-job shithead has made all day!' or words to that effect. 'Just make sure that he doesn't fuck up the parade in the process!'

So, after lunch, I asked my brother Mark, who just happened to be doing his national service at the army base and who'd met my aircraft when we'd landed, to arrange a two-way radio connection between my chopper and the rugby stadium so I could keep abreast of the parade's progress and time my arrival to coincide precisely with its conclusion.

After doing a check of the communications link between my helicopter and his handheld radio transceiver, and making sure it worked, Mark left to go to the stadium. I waited, smiling quietly to myself, chuffed that through my personal ingenuity I might still rescue a sticky situation and get the general home to Pretoria without further delay, hopefully staving off any punitive reaction from him along the way.

The first sign of impending trouble occurred when I tried to call my brother over the radio at the stadium but failed to make contact with him. I tried numerous times, without any success, so, being a resourceful chap, I made another plan.

I called out to a group of pongo corporals who were standing close by, one of whom had *spoorsnyer* (tracker) flashes on his shoulders and asked them to indicate to me exactly where the rugby stadium was in relation to where we were parked. The tracker, puffing his chest out confidently, pointed in the direction of the stadium and said, 'It are about three clicks (kilometres) that way, Lieutenant!'

'Are you sure?' I asked.

'I grew big in Amsterdam, Lieutenant. Of course I am,' he stated categorically and with great indignation.

Satisfied that I had got the best directions possible, from the person best qualified to give them, my revised plan to neatly pluck the general up from his current position now focused on my avoiding, at all costs, flying over the stadium during the general's parade. When I gauged that the parade was well under way, I would take off, give the stadium a very, *very* wide berth and climb up to, and land on, one of the many hills that surround the town of Amsterdam, from where I could view proceedings down in the rugby stadium far below.

After taking off at what I estimated to be the appropriate time, I turned at right angles to the direction shown by the resident tracker corporal and proceeded, at slightly above treetop height (around 35 metres above ground level), towards a distant hill.

So, there we were, cruising along and enjoying the view when suddenly, looking down, I saw a vast sea of startled and wide-eyed faces, 10 000 of them I was told later, sitting shoulder to shoulder on the tiered seating of the main grandstand of the Amsterdam rugby stadium. They were all looking up at me, some with their hands over their ears to block the deafening screech of the 880-shaft-horsepower Alo III, passing just a few metres above their heads.

I'm no rocket scientist, but I generally know when I am in the wrong place at the wrong time. In the Border War, when someone shot at me with ill intent, the pace at which events unfolded always instantly slowed down to super slow motion.

The same thing happened at that moment.

Each detail of the scenery now passing so agonisingly slowly below was scorched into my mind. Blind panic took hold as my eyes moved from the sea of faces across to the athletics track running around the periphery of the rugby field and then on to the small VIP platform facing the massive crowd and upon which sat Amsterdam's mayor, his wife, the base's OC and the colonel.

AWOL, count 2.

Standing at the rostrum, a metre or two from the other VIPs, was the general. His face was contorted by a terrible rage. I could see flecks of foamy spittle and his jaws were open so wide that I could almost see the remains of his lunch.

'*Hier kom kak* (Here comes shit),' said Johnny.

Making my untimely intrusion a lot worse was the fact that the general had been about to conclude his speech. To rub salt into the festering wound caused by my ceremony-destroying fly-by, after the Alo had departed the scene the general had resumed his oration, but not a single person in the audience paid him any further heed. Instead, they fixed their eyes on my little bird while I sought a suitable hilltop perch. There is little that will piss off an entertainer more than losing his audience as he is about to deliver the closing pitch.

Insubordination, count 5, brought the total number of charges to ten.

I landed on the hilltop, but there was not much said between Johnny and me. I stopped the rotor blades from spinning but left the engine at flight idle and waited until the parade started its closing act, the general salute. Then I got things going again, took off and swept down the hillside towards the rugby stadium.

To add further complication to an already calamitous day, positioning the Alo for its final approach and landing into the wind, like any well-trained pilot would and must do, necessitated my flying directly over the heads of the troops marching off the parade ground.

Perhaps I should have increased the height above them to 30 to 40 feet (9 to 12 metres), but I figured that might put me in a dangerous position should the engine fail at that point, so I flew over the departing parade at a height of no more than 12 feet (3.6 metres) or so. The resulting chaos, as berets were scattered to the four winds and the well-ordered ranks of young soldiers disintegrated, did not please the general.

Malicious Damage to State Property, count 2.

As I slowed to a crawl in preparation for landing in front of the VIP platform, a cloud of tinder-dry flakes of Kikuyu grass mixed with fine red dust swept up by the rotor wash instantly robbed me of any visual references whatsoever. To avoid a serious situation from developing in the vertigo-inducing conditions, I immediately reduced engine power and thumped the Alo onto the ground, still in one piece and not hard enough to damage it.

My brother, who had managed to scramble to the edge of the rugby field, where he had a clear view of the events unfolding in the stadium proper, later told me that the cloud of grass and dust completely filled the stadium. From my vantage point in the cockpit I could see little, but deep down I knew then that I was unlikely to get away lightly with what had just happened.

As the choking fog of dust and grass slowly cleared, I espied the general making his way to the aircraft, coughing and spluttering madly. I knew it was him only because I recognised the spectacles on his face and the murderous anger in his eyes. Gone were the shiny rank insignia, the buffed shine on his shoes; the rest of him was just red dust and tiny flakes of Kikuyu grass. Even his teeth were red …

Malicious Damage to State Property, count 3.

I could clearly hear his roaring tirade above the screech of the Alo's engine, and I knew instinctively that he wasn't complimenting me on my skill at landing the aircraft in zero-zero conditions (when a pilot cannot see his hand in front of his face, but the sun is still shining).

Under the circumstances, Johnny Smith really shouldn't have let the general near the aircraft, let alone allow him to board, but in Johnny's defence, I don't think he could have stopped the general if he'd shot him with a portable G5 cannon. The general launched himself into the Alo's passenger compartment and grabbed me by the throat, pulling me against the back of my seat and trying his level best to throttle the life out of me. His aide quickly intervened and pulled him away.

Startled by this conduct unbecoming of a senior rank, I half-turned in my seat to prevent further attack and observed the colonel, fortunately a man of some physical stature, with his arms wrapped around the general, restraining him from resuming his assault on me.

How it got there I do not know, but when I looked at my right hand I observed a large number 1 socket wrench in it, probably placed there by Johnny. I may then have waved it in a marginally threatening manner in the direction of the general, but I felt justified in doing so as my feelings (and throat) had been hurt.

Insubordination, count 7. If I'd pushed things, I believe that the general's assault on me might have made the charge count 13–1.

Then I looked at the colonel's face and saw that he was trying hard, but unsuccessfully, to suppress hysterical laughter. His shoulders were shaking. Tears formed in his eyes and then leaked out, making squiggly furrows through the red dust caking his face.

I started to giggle, Johnny started to giggle and the colonel, turning away from the general, began shaking with laughter, unseen by his boss. The general was still focusing all his energy and vehemence on me. Before I could lower the visor on my helmet sufficiently to shield my face, the general uttered the final words he was to say to me on that fateful day:

'Wipe that fucking smile off your fucking face!'

This I was unable to do, which brought about Disobeying a Lawful Command, count 3, taking the final tally of charges to 14.

Then, without warning, the general collapsed, utterly spent, on the back seat of my little helicopter, from where he stared at the passing scenery for the next two hours as we flew back to Pretoria, no doubt carefully plotting his revenge.

*

Two days after returning from my eventful day trip to Amsterdam, I was telephonically requested to drop by the AFB Swartkop legal office for a 'chat' with the legal officer – generally a national serviceman with a law degree – with the proviso that I 'make time to do so today, please'.

Mildly perturbed, I headed down to the base legal office on auto-pilot. I'd been a regular visitor – there was a very pretty girl who worked there – and knew the way in my sleep. On the way, I got to thinking that perhaps the colonel from the Amsterdam trip had spilt the beans on his anger-management-needy boss and that I was required to make a statement as a witness.

For all intents and purposes the legal officer was the SAAF's local prosecutor in what were called 'summary trials' (comparable to misdemeanour trials in a magistrate's court). He was a gravely serious chap who wore the insignia of a captain, an unusual rank for a national serviceman, and he seemed new to the post, as I'd never met him before.

But, belying his undertaker-like demeanour, he introduced himself, shook my hand warmly and invited me into his office.

The next moment he said, 'Tut, tut, tut, tut. What in devil's name are we going to do about these charges, Lieutenant?'

'What charge ... I mean, charges?' I stammered.

Dispensing with any further informality and friendliness, he suddenly barked, like a Gestapo interrogator, 'Are you the Lieutenant Stephen Pierre Joubert, force number 74257684PE, who was tasked with flying General H and his aide to and from Amsterdam, Transvaal, in an Alouette III helicopter, serial number 519, on 14 June 1981?'

'That sounds like me. Yes,' I replied hesitantly.

'Do you deny or accept that on said day, with said passengers, in and around said aircraft, you wilfully and with malice aforethought committed a series of offences, 14 in total, that combined to jeopardise the integrity, credibility and standing of the aforementioned general and his aide, caused malicious damage to property belonging to the South African state and that you behaved in a manner unbefitting an officer and gentleman in the South African Air Force?'

'Fourteen charges! Fourteen fucking charges? Are you out of your mind?' I screamed before panic closed my throat and stopped me from breathing.

'Yes, 14 charges have been filed against you by General Hanekom, and I have been personally appointed by him to prosecute you to the full extent of military law. The charges are as follows.'

I sat down and listened as he went through each and every charge. At one stage, I think it was the point at which the general had demanded that I put on the heater and I'd refused (Disobeying a Lawful Command, count 2), I chuckled nervously, which brought an angry response.

'Do you think that this is a laughing matter, Lieutenant? With me prosecuting your sorry ass, you will be lucky to get out of this with your scrotum still attached to your torso!' he said sternly.

By the time he had read out the final charge, I had traversed the full range of emotions from hysteria and maniacal mirth to denial and panic before finally settling on fury. I had also decided that the SAAF could kiss my lily-white backside goodbye and that I'd go directly to my bank manager (I didn't actually have one, having only a building society account into which my wealth, or lack of it, was concentrated) and borrow the R20 000 or so I'd need to buy myself out of what remained of my ten-year short-service contract and resign my commission.

I was beside myself with anger at the 17 Squadron hierarchy, all Border War colleagues, who'd made not the slightest attempt to insert themselves between me and the general, nor to offer me moral support, nor even to ask me what had happened.

'Fuck it,' I thought, 'these are guys that I have trusted to keep me alive, who have been able to totally depend on me to reciprocate whenever required, who have lived with me and got drunk with me and who I thought would always have my back, and me theirs, and this is how quickly they disappear when I need them?'

So, when he'd spelt out in the finest detail, as he'd done with the other 13 charges, the last count under which I'd been charged, the legal officer asked, 'How will you plead to these charges, Lieutenant?'

I replied with an impulsivity born of blind rage, youthful indignation and bitter disappointment.

'Find me guilty on all counts and ... and ... fuck the lot of you!'

I stormed out of his office.

*

My appointment with the manager of a Barclays Bank branch didn't go as well as I'd hoped. He laughed out loud when I told him that I wanted to borrow R20 000 from the bank to pay the SAAF back for the millions (even in those days it cost millions to train an Air Force pilot) spent on training me.

'Get over it,' he said, before urging me, in a fatherly way, to think very, very carefully about trashing my career while in a state of such aggravation.

Two days passed before I'd calmed down enough to objectively contemplate my predicament and take the long walk down to the legal office to change my plea and put on record a more balanced version of events than that offered by the general.

'Sorry, no can do,' said the legal officer brightly, when I eventually got an audience with him. 'In military law, once you have pleaded guilty to the charges, you may not retract your plea, but don't worry, at the summary trial itself, you will have plenty of opportunity to offer evidence in mitigation of sentence.'

I never checked whether this was actually the case or whether he was just disinclined to redo all the paperwork – probably the latter – but I left his office and started to work on my mitigation arguments.

The summary trial took place the following week in the office of AFB Swartkop's OC, the legendary Colonel Jimmy 'JJ' Groenewald, who, as luck would have it, was appointed as the presiding officer (the judge). He was one of the last of the Second World War pilots still serving in the SAAF in a full-time capacity. At the start of formalities, I think he quickly came to the conclusion that this was anything but a cut-and-dried case of a junior officer overstepping the mark.

I had never been in his hallowed presence before, so I was nervous beyond description as I marched into his office to begin the hearing, which the legal officer estimated would 'take only 30 minutes or so. You have, after all, pleaded guilty to all 14 charges and all you have with which to defend yourself is your mitigation statement.'

After opening by repeating the charges, every bloody one of them, the legal officer told Colonel Groenewald that I'd pleaded guilty to all charges and that all he needed to do was issue appropriate punishment for my multiple sins.

'I … I'd like to say something before you do that, Colonel,' I interrupted.

'Go ahead then,' Colonel Groenewald said.

Using every trick in the book to demonstrate my complete innocence, I launched into a long and finely detailed account of the comedy of factors, coincidences and misunderstandings that had played out during that fateful nine-hour trip. In the end, I spent almost two and a half hours in 'mitigating' my sentence.

At the point where I described General Hanekom emerging from the impenetrable cloud of dust and grass on the Amsterdam rugby field, Colonel Groenewald got out of his chair and sat on the floor, pulling up his knees to his chest as he laughed and laughed until the tears rolled in torrents down his cheeks. When I was finally done with the tale, I asked him if I could visit the gents.

By the time I returned to his office, he'd ordered that tea be brought for us. Then he asked the legal officer to wait outside to be summoned, 'which might take a while', he added.

'In all my years—' he started to say when we were alone, before doubling up with laughter again until he lost his breath.

Finally, and this took quite a while (believe me), he became serious and said, 'My boy, there is no doubt in my mind that you are completely without guilt on all the charges. My concern is that you never professed your innocence from the start. Why not?'

I told him about the anger I'd felt when the charges were levelled at me and the disappointment at the lack of support offered by the squadron hierarchy. He promised that he'd deal with that issue, and I have no doubt that he did. I never again heard of a young pilot being left in the lurch when he needed support.

'But, practically, you and I need to box very clever now,' he went on. 'General Hanekom is aware that you are answering to his charges today, and I am under strict orders to report on the outcome to him the moment these proceedings end. I think that we have two options to properly resolve this matter. The first will have me finding you not guilty on all charges—'

I interrupted him in mid-sentence: 'I really like that option, Colonel.'

'But I suggest you listen to option two before you make your final choice,' he continued. 'If I find you innocent, as I should, I can assure you that General H will not accept my findings and that he will then use all of his considerable influence to hound you ceaselessly until the day you depart the SAAF and probably even beyond that.'

Stunned at this revelation, I said glumly, 'I'm pretty stuffed, aren't I, sir? What is option two?'

'Not necessarily,' replied Groenewald. 'What I suggest is that I find you guilty on all 14 charges, state on the trial report that I categorically reject any of your arguments in mitigation, and then I hand out the harshest possible punishment that the MDC allows, on each count.'

I went pale.

'With all due respect, I don't think I'm a great fan of option two, sir,' I said, visions of having to take up permanent residence in the orderly officer's room, scrubbing toilets and staying a second lieutenant until I retired swamping my imagination.

'But here's the kicker,' he said. 'If you choose option two, I promise you faithfully that I won't allow a single page of paperwork relating to this matter ever to leave my office or to become attached to your personal file. In fact, once I've reported to General H that you have been severely dealt with, and that you are unlikely to see the light of day for years to come, I will personally shred every single document involved. Please trust me. I will not let you down.'

Thus, the matter was settled. We shook hands and he invited the legal officer to rejoin us.

With a sternness that was almost comical, Colonel Groenewald then read out his contrived judgments and followed these with the applicable maximum sentences under each count. As he read out the severe punishments, he never once displayed a hint of understanding, nor even a single acknowledgement, of the mitigating factors that I had so passionately and eloquently presented.

I was lashed mercilessly by Colonel Groenewald, who brought down a whole slew of fines, extra duties, delayed promotion and even two years' denial of Christmas bonus on my miserable head.

But, try as I might, I still couldn't hide the grin that wrapped around my face from ear to ear, nor fully mute the odd chuckle as a particularly harsh censure was handed down. I could see the legal officer struggling to comprehend. I suspect he began to cotton on right at the end, as I was leaving the trial venue, when Colonel Groenewald told him to leave the processing of the paperwork up to him.

'After all,' Groenewald said, 'I've not got much else to do.'

Years later, I had occasion to draw my personal file and peruse it closely.

There was not a single reference to the 'Amsterdam incident'.

But then, you already knew that, didn't you?

9
Losing faith

In December 1980, I got married. I had known Desiree for only nine months, at least six of which I had spent on tours in the bush. In the year after we tied the knot, I was home for only four months in total.

It should surprise no one that this was not the basis for a happy-ever-after fairy tale. Although we both tried our best to make it work, the marriage ended after ten years. However, it did produce a gift of incalculable value to the two of us, our daughter Tamarin.

The 'Amsterdam incident', or rather its aftermath, fundamentally changed something in me, although I was not consciously aware of the seismic shift at the time or for many years afterwards. When I look back now, I see that it blew away any ideals I still harboured that all my colleagues had my back in times of strife. At the same time, it led me to attach far greater value to the friendships built with the chaps upon whom I knew I could depend.

As is the case with most operational squadrons, 17 Squadron had a pool of pilots who formed the 'inner sanctum', with the rest on the periphery. I was undoubtedly part of the latter grouping, who were still useful but less likely to be given the peach assignments or unwavering support. This 'placing' even extended to one's family.

For instance, once while I was away on a tour, my brand-new wife was invited to a tea party for the wives of the squadron's pilots. She arrived and was greeted warmly by the hostess, but soon noticed that many wives were not present. She also picked up that the missing wives were exclusively those whose home language, like ours, was English. When Desiree asked the hostess where the missing wives might be, she was told by the giggling lady that she had 'forgotten to invite the English wives'.

It seemed that the tea-party planner had erroneously deduced that Joubert was an Afrikaans surname and added Desiree's name to the guest list.

*

During one of my tours to the Border, again based in Ondangwa, I was one of the gunship pilots in a two-ship formation that was tasked to provide close air support to an army reconnaissance operation taking place 25 kilometres into Angola just north of the Namacunde–Chiede road.

The other pilot was Neil McCall. We were to stand by at the old army base at Etale. As we climbed out of our aircraft after landing, we could hear the distant sound of mortars and rifle fire. We immediately got airborne and headed for the fight.

When we got to the scene, it was carnage.

It seems that an army patrol, based at Etale and mounted on horseback, had been ambushed by a large group of PLAN soldiers. This was unusual as, up to then, PLAN had been inclined to avoid contact with SADF forces, particularly when operating on Namibian soil.

There were some fatalities and a handful of our soldiers had been badly injured in the ambush, which ended as soon as the sounds of the approaching choppers could be heard by those on the ground. As was their usual practice, the PLAN soldiers bombshelled as soon as the attack was over.

Unfortunately for the PLAN guys that day, the site they'd chosen for the ambush lay in a large patch of dense bush, surrounded to the east, south and west by open salt pans. Only those who scarpered to the north, as most of them did, were assured of having overhead tree cover as they made good their escape.

Those who went south were easily tracked and dealt with in an operation that lasted most of the day. Neil McCall or me, or both of us, provided air support to the ground troops who swept through the area. As one of our pair of gunships would run low on fuel, the pilot would depart the scene and go to Etale to refuel, rearm and eat/drink before returning to relieve the other crew.

Finally, the action petered out and I returned to Etale. As I walked from my aircraft to the ops tent, I passed the main helipad, where the bodies of the dead PLAN soldiers had been placed. The bodies were being put into body bags for transportation by Puma to Oshakati, where I assumed they'd be identified, processed and afforded a dignified burial.

Just then, a youngish army major marched a group of around 30 young national servicemen or three-month campers (I never did find out which) up to the dead PLAN soldiers and began shouting insults at the bodies, his face contorted and angry, veins sticking prominently out of his sunburnt neck. My anger immediately rocketed off the charts, and when he made a move as if to kick one of them, something in me snapped.

During the months and years of lying, gin-depressed but still wide-awake into the small hours, in my mosquito-net-shielded cocoon, I had occasionally envisioned being shot down and killed inside enemy territory. This morbid image had evoked in me a hope, never voiced aloud to anyone, that if this ever happened, and I truly hoped it wouldn't, that my body at least be treated with respect by those who gained custody of it.

I believed implicitly that such courtesy should work both ways, and in my sudden rage I saw this jumped-up tosser of a major, in attempting to impress his troops, violate the dignity of fallen military men. Before I could be stopped, or stop myself, I grabbed the major by the throat and pinned him up against a prefabricated concrete wall. I was so livid, so furious, that I was unable to speak, and just stared into his shocked eyes.

After a few seconds, some other chaps pinned my arms against my sides and I had to let him go and walk away. I think he ran after me and tried to take the issue further, but wiser heads intervened and prevented further confrontation.

I can't remember any more of what subsequently happened, if anything, other than that I was extraordinarily tired afterwards.

A day or so later, the four-man reconnaissance group who had originally been standing by at Etale to help, were themselves attacked while hiding out in the heat of the day in a patch of bush situated in the middle of a *shona* 30 kilometres into Angola.

Neil and I scrambled to help them and we arrived over their position 20 minutes later.

Of the original four in the recce group, only two white officers remained. The other two, being Ovambo tribesmen and able to melt into the local landscape, had already managed to make good their escape by the time we arrived.

Both men had been wounded, and even though we were in gunships in the sky above them, they were still taking heavy fire from the FAPLA troops who'd found them. The FAPLA contingent had dug into secure cover immediately west of the two recces, and we were unable to see their positions in the heavy bush. Nevertheless, we laid down covering fire, hoping to keep them from advancing on our guys.

Neil suggested to me that I descend, land and pick up one of the guys on the ground while he gave me covering fire. When I had done so and was again airborne, I could provide cover for him to pick up the remaining recce and then we could get out of there. He also suggested that I jettison my 20 mm cannon if I found that my gunship was too heavy to take off with the additional weight of a passenger. I realised that this would leave him extremely vulnerable to enemy fire when he went in, but he told me that it was a chance he was willing to take.

After planning my approach to the LZ, and just as I was starting my descent, the radio crackled into life. A formation of two Pumas with medical personnel aboard reported that they were just a few minutes out, and that our two gunships were to remain on station and make certain that enemy fire was suppressed while they extracted the wounded recces.

The extraction proceeded without further incident.

Two days after that, our two gunships were called out to an army base called Elundu to provide air support to an imminent punch-up between a small stick (four to six men) of PLAN soldiers and some SADF infantry based at Elundu, who were following their tracks ever more closely.

We were soon to discover that the main body of the 120-strong group of PLAN fighters, which had ambushed the mounted army patrol near Etale just days earlier, had regrouped and were intent on creating havoc in Ovamboland by taking on the SADF directly. This level of aggression was unheard of and, as such, totally unexpected.

The main PLAN body, using local informants to establish the whereabouts of a 20-strong army patrol, were lying in wait in an ambush position on a small road about eight kilometres east of the Elundu base. They had earlier sent out a stick of four soldiers to walk ahead of the army patrol and lure them into the ambush.

At around 14h00 Neil and I were in the operations room at the Elundu base listening to events unfold on the radio when the patrol walked into the ambush and bullets, mortars and RPG-7s started to fly. As we ran out of the operations room, Neil, being taller than me, ran straight into a piece of angle iron that framed the exit from the underground structure. The impact opened a large wound on his forehead that required immediate attention from the base doctor, so I was forced to proceed to the contact scene on my own and he'd follow as soon as he could.

When I arrived, I had a clear view of our soldiers pinned down on the ground while mortars exploded among them. One fellow had been shot dead in the initial fusillade from the enemy and another had been shot in the stomach. All of them had dug holes into the soft sand with their hands and were trying to be as unobtrusive as humanly possible.

As normal, the arrival of a gunship overhead caused enemy fire to cease immediately. With the patrol commander giving me information over the radio about the direction from which the attack had come and my visual assessment, I knew that it was unlikely that the aggressors had departed the scene. So, while attempting to ignite the dense dry bush around the enemy positions with HE rounds from the 20 mm, which sometimes work like incendiaries, I kept telling the friendlies on the ground to remain in their positions until the all clear could be sounded.

I don't know how long I orbited the scene, fruitlessly searching for movement or visual anomalies that would reveal the positions of the PLAN soldiers. Then, out of the corner of my eye, I saw a movement among the pinned-down patrol as one of them stood up to go to the aid of the wounded man. The would-be rescuer was immediately shot dead by an enemy sniper.

'For fuck's sakes, stay down until I give the all clear!' I screamed over the radio at the patrol, frustration and helplessness threatening to overwhelm me.

The exasperation grew exponentially as I searched each square metre of the surrounding bush, in vain, for the hidden enemy troops.

There was no more firing after that one shot. When Neil arrived, head stitched up, we were finally able to declare the scene safe and get help to those who needed it. For the next couple of hours, we took turns to move our own patrols into the area to cut off the escape routes of the PLAN soldiers involved in the earlier ambush.

The shadows were already quite long, and I estimate that it was around 17h00, when I looked down and saw a group of around 30 uniformed soldiers walking through the bush. They were looking up at me as I circled them. None of our patrols was supposed to be where these guys were, and there was something unusual about the way they looked or the way they were walking – I couldn't put my finger on it.

I made a number of radio calls asking for the patrol below me to please identify themselves. Nothing. Not a peep. Then I asked that all the patrols in the area, seven or eight in total, make sure that their members were present and accounted for. They all confirmed that they were and that none were below my circling chopper.

Still unsure, and obviously completely unwilling to attack my own troops with a 20 mm cannon, I decided to take a closer look and descended to a height of around 150 metres.

Suddenly, from the edge of the group walking below me, I saw a man go down on one knee and point something up at my gunship. This was followed by a flash as the RPG-7 he was holding was fired. Then all hell broke loose. My abiding memory is of the curved magazines of the AK-47s as everyone opened fire on my poor little helicopter.

The 20 mm immediately began its staccato beat as my flight engineer opened up with repeated two-to-three-shot bursts at the rapidly dispersing enemy below. I saw a number of them struck and fall to the ground. Then the 20 mm jammed. By the time the flight engineer had cleared the obstruction, the balance of the enemy force had disappeared.

From the firing of the RPG at my gunship to the jamming of our 20 mm perhaps 20 to 30 seconds had elapsed. Although it was late in the day to do so, I called in some Pumas that had just arrived to drop reaction-force stopper groups on the ground, in an attempt to box the enemy in.

No more than a few minutes after my blazing encounter with the PLAN group, one of the Pumas passed below me, travelling from my 5 o'clock to 11 o'clock. From behind and directly underneath me there suddenly appeared a bright red dot trailing black smoke, the undeniable signature of another RPG-7 projectile, which was chasing the departing Puma and rapidly gaining on it.

At the last possible moment, the Puma seemed quickly to lift its tail boom, like a girl raising her long skirts when jumping over a spider on the ground. The lethal chunk of Russian widowmaker missed it by only a few inches.

As it did so, I heard the pilot of the Puma shout, 'Yikes! That was close.'

*

My final encounter with this unusual group of PLAN soldiers was a few days later when they ambushed a convoy of supply vehicles on Fernando's Road between Oshigambo and Eenhana. The convoy protection detail consisted of some young national servicemen who'd been in the bush only a few days.

Again, our gunship formation just happened to be in the vicinity and we arrived overhead quite quickly, within ten minutes or so of the attack. We were confronted with utter carnage and indescribable terror on the part of the survivors. I recall that it took quite a while to calm a young man who was screaming hysterically into the handset of the ground-to-air radio, which was still attached to his friend, a 17-year-old boy who'd been fatally wounded in the opening salvo of the attack.

Although the panic-stricken infantrymen had attempted to drive out of the ambush when they realised what was happening, this frantic course of action unknowingly compromised their convoy's defensive integrity, as all the vehicles were so comprehensively shot up by the well-organised attackers that they managed only to get a short distance down the road before breaking down, each quite a way from the next, halting any further escape.

Some months later I was in a pub at the Army Battle School in Lohatla when a young national service officer approached me, having somehow recognised me, and offered to buy me a drink. He told me that he'd been involved in the ambush, and that his abject terror had been born of the very real prospect that the enemy would overrun the almost defenceless disabled vehicles and slaughter all the survivors. The fortuitous arrival of our two gunships, however, scuppered the PLAN objectives, and the attackers had dispersed into the bush. The young officer told me that the 'whop-whopping' of the rotors and the noise of the engines as the two Alos arrived overhead was the sweetest sound he'd ever heard. It was only then that his fear had started to abate.

He was 19 years old at the time.

*

In April 1981, an operation was planned to hit a PLAN base just east of Xangongo (formerly Vila Roçadas), and I was one of the chopper pilots chosen to participate. The operation started unremarkably with two gunships flown by Paul Dore and Paul Downer (nicknamed 'the two Pauls') flying to Cuamato, a hamlet around 60 kilometres inside Angola.

When not occupied by invading SADF forces, Cuamato was usually the base for a small contingent of FAPLA troops. Once overhead, the two Pauls fired short bursts from their 20 mm cannons into the middle of the main street. This had become relatively standard practice (never a good thing in war) and had previously always led to the FAPLA soldiers stationed there immediately vacating the village and heading for safety some distance to the north.

When the FAPLA soldiers were clear of the area, Puma helicopters would bring in a large force of SADF men and equipment to set up the ops headquarters and the rest of the Alos would land there too. The force would then invariably be joined by the armoured contingent, who had driven off-road to Cuamato in their Ratels and Elands from inside Ovamboland.

Cuamato was a pretty place, with nice trees, a good supply of potable water and a number of buildings that were still usable. This was why the SADF regularly chose it as the forward staging post for short-duration raids on PLAN camps in southern Angola.

At roughly 14h00 on that first day, and about three kilometres north of Cuamato, a patrol of 20 or so SADF soldiers who had been tasked with reconnoitring the area to the north of the village walked unexpectedly into a well-defended FAPLA camp containing a few hundred soldiers. The FAPLA contingent opened fire on the patrol with anti-aircraft weapons and killed two of our infantrymen.

The two Pauls immediately got airborne to offer air support to the troops trapped on the ground. They were soon joined by two more gunships that had been sent to the scene. The two Pauls were operating below a sizeable cloud of smoke and exploding anti-aircraft projectiles but were seemingly unaware of the intensity of the FAPLA reaction to their presence.

At dusk, when the infantrymen who'd been trapped since the start of the contact were finally able to withdraw, the two Pauls and the other two gunships returned to overnight at Ombalantu, which was situated just inside South West Africa. There, they were joined by another four gunships and a .303-equipped Alo III trooper (able to carry a crew of two and a maximum of three passengers), which would carry the battle commander in the following day's ops and would be flown by me. That night, in the Ombalantu pub, we heard how, as they neared Cuamato in the fading light of the late afternoon, it had looked like a scene from a war film.

Early the next morning, the nine Alos left Ombalantu and arrived at Cuamato just before sunrise. A quick local intelligence update informed us that during the night there had been a lot of vehicle movement from the direction of the FAPLA positions. Based on past experience, it was likely that FAPLA had used the night hours to pull back rather than risk any further confrontation with the SADF.

Our formation of eight gunships and my trooper got airborne just as the sun peeked over the easterly horizon, and we headed at treetop height for the original PLAN base target around 25 kilometres away. As we approached just to the east of the FAPLA positions that had caused so many problems the previous day, our formation leader, Lieutenant Billy Port, began describing to the five of us who'd not been there the day before exactly where the FAPLA camp was located.

The radio call went something like this: 'Okay, okes, you see the fence of dried bushes coming up – that is the southern border of the camp. The northern border is where the thick bush starts and the headquarters is where—'

He didn't finish the sentence.

Without warning, a whole barrage of FAPLA weaponry opened fire on us from dug-in positions along a 200-metre-long line of trenches and camouflaged structures, situated roughly in the middle of the FAPLA camp. One moment there was nothing happening, and the next it was as if a massive warehouse filled with fireworks had spontaneously ignited.

Fortunately, we were already as close to the ground as it was possible to get and so were able to dodge the barrage. Immediately, the plan to attack the original PLAN objective was put on ice and we spent the rest of the morning, supported by ground-attack Mirages and Impalas, in subduing the FAPLA base.

In the afternoon, as the overrun FAPLA base was being swept by our ground troops, I flew well-known war correspondent and photographer Al J Venter around the area to get an idea of the scale, orientation and layout of the battlefield. He later used photographs taken that day in his book *The Chopper Boys*.

After I dropped him off at Cuamato, I took two brigadiers, one of whom was Bossie Huyser, the SAAF commanding officer in South West Africa, to the FAPLA camp. After switching off the engine, the flight engineer disappeared into the maze of trenches to look for an AK-47 for personal use. (All combat aircrew could choose what weapons they wanted to include in their on-board survival equipment, and the AK-47 was a preferred choice. It could always be relied on to fire when needed, irrespective of any abuse it might have suffered. We had all seen videos of an AK-47 that had been immersed in mud for six months being lifted out of the corrosive goo and immediately cocked and fired.)

I attached myself to the two brigs but had the (in my case) rare foresight to carry my own AK-47 with twin magazines taped together while we strolled along inspecting the overrun FAPLA camp. About ten metres in front of us, a young sapper carrying a metal detector was preparing to negotiate the steep entrance to one of the many underground bunkers when, from within the bunker, a FAPLA soldier who was hiding there shot him. The force of the AK-47 bullet lifted the sapper clean off his feet and catapulted him backwards as if he'd been snatched by a giant invisible hand.

We rushed forward and pulled the seriously wounded young man out of harm's way. The area around us suddenly bristled with activity as soldiers emptied entire magazines into any bunker entrance they could find.

Twenty metres away, the commander of the ground troops, a Major Blaauw, shouted forcefully, 'Make sure that all the bunkers are clean!' before he dashed forward, pulled the safety pin from a fragmentation grenade and tossed it into a bunker in front of him.

He was standing in front of the entrance to the bunker when the grenade exploded inside with a muffled thump. A huge tongue of flame blasted out of the entrance and completely engulfed him, searing any exposed flesh and melting the hair on his head so that it resembled a shiny skullcap.

Without hesitation, I turned and headed at breakneck speed for my Alo. My mind was in a frantic whirl, but then time seemed to slow, as it did when the screws were on. I shouted loudly for medical personnel to attend to the casualties and to bring them to the chopper as soon as they could be moved so that I could fly them both to Cuamato. From there, the Pumas could get them to expert medical care at Oshakati or Ondangwa.

Then I yelled for my engineer, Theo Munroe, to get the hell out of whatever trenches he was in and get back to the Alo III trooper. Lastly, I called for the two brigadiers to stay put at the LZ, as I would return to collect them after I'd done the casualty evacuation. Before long, both the major and the sapper were bundled aboard and we took off for Cuamato, barely three kilometres away.

The indelible memory that I have of that two-minute flight is of Major Blaauw, clearly in a state of shock, rubbing the top of his skull where the charred blob of molten goo that had been his hair had adhered. This action caused the blob to break apart into small pieces that floated all around the cockpit. A piece found its way into one of my nostrils and I still shudder and retch when I recall the unbelievably acrid odour.

I spent another night at Ombalantu, during which I swapped the trooper for a gunship from one of the Alo pilots who was going home. Before dawn, our formation of eight gunships returned to Cuamato, all of us absolutely certain that the FAPLA force, or any survivors of the previous afternoon's sweep, would have left the scene during the night. They'd taken an awful pounding and would likely want to get as far away from the SADF as possible.

We still intended to hit the original PLAN target that morning.

But, just as the Alo formation came in to land at Cuamato, one behind the other, the two lead aircraft peeled off and started to climb up to their operating height of 800 feet (250 metres). They had been instructed to provide top cover for a couple of Pumas that were about to uplift a 20-strong group of our troops who had been lying in ambush throughout the night next to the road leading from the FAPLA camp to Cuamato.

They were no more than a few hundred feet above the ground when the air around them suddenly erupted with hundreds of small explosions originating from Russian-made ZSU 23-4 anti-aircraft guns. From our vantage point in the other six gunships that had just landed, we could clearly see that they were in a lot of trouble. Their chances of surviving the heavy barrage seemed decidedly small.

But both pilots instinctively dived for the cover of the vegetation as the trail of radar-guided anti-aircraft fire followed them right down to the tops of the trees. In fact, the tail boom of one of the two choppers hit the trees while evading the lethal fire, but the pilot still managed to maintain control of his aircraft.

No one argued when, minutes later, all choppers, Alos and Pumas alike, were instructed to get the hell out of Cuamato and head for a patch of land around ten kilometres to the east, which would serve as a temporary HAA until a better course of action could be formulated. At the time, I could not recall any occasion when enemy activity had forced the SADF to leave anywhere it had claimed as its base of operations, and a feeling of great disquiet took root in my belly.

We reached the temporary HAA without further incident and took stock of the situation.

At around lunchtime on the same day, a 32 Battalion patrol radioed that they were holed up, resting through the heat of the day, in a thick patch of bush on the edge of a *shona* around 15 kilometres northeast of our position, and that they could hear the sounds of a convoy of enemy vehicles coming in their direction, obviously searching for them.

Six gunships were immediately scrambled, with me at the rear as tail-end-Charlie. At the last possible moment before I took off, the OC of 32 Battalion, Commandant Deon 'Jelly babes' Ferreira, jumped into my aircraft and sat on the floor in the front left of the Alo, insisting that I allow him to tag along for the anticipated 'turkey shoot'.

On the approach to the imminent contact I remember being quite excited at the prospect of taking on a convoy of vehicles, given my previous experience of the tanker along the Kunene River. As we closed in on the target, the leader of the 32 Battalion patrol, observing events from his refuge on the ground, whispered on the radio that he could clearly see the vehicles, which were now stopped on the edge of the *shona*, 200 metres from his position.

With around two kilometres to go to the target, the pilot leading our gunship formation pitched the nose of his chopper upwards and began a right-hand climbing turn. The rest of us strung out behind him to form a left-orbit circle around the target vehicles, which I could clearly see as soon as my gunship cleared the tops of the trees.

I was climbing through around 130 metres above the trees when the leader of the army patrol concealed in the bush alongside the *shona* suddenly broke radio silence and shouted, the anguish in his voice rising with each word, 'They've taken the tarpaulins off the back of the trucks. Shit. They've got missiles. Gunships, get the fuck out of here!'

I had no time to react before the ground-to-air SAM-7 missiles started to streak away from the launchers around the GAZ trucks, and great clouds of white smoke from the ignition of the rocket motors rapidly obscured my view of the vehicles.

For a moment, I was mesmerised by the activity on the ground, and the gravity of the situation had not yet dawned on me when the leader of our formation shouted, 'Steve, get down on the trees, you dumb idiot, or you will be shot down!'

Of the 17 SAM-7s fired at our formation in less than 20 seconds, 16 of them, failing to lock on to a target, spiralled off harmlessly into the sky.

The remaining missile, however, probably fired by a more patient operator, streaked directly for my gunship, probably because I had reacted far too slowly to avoid it. When I saw it heading for me, my perspective somehow shifted from sitting in the pilot's seat of the Alo to watching the events unfold from a position outside the aircraft, about five metres in front and to the right of the nose.

In my mind's eye, I can still see the missile leaving the launcher tube near the back of the truck.

I see the moment, just a split second later, when the rocket motor ignites and a great cloud of white smoke forms behind the missile.

I see the approaching metallic tube, with its staring glass eye, waggle slightly as it searches for an infrared light source on my gunship.

I see it nod its head almost imperceptibly as it locks onto a shiny spot on the Alo.

By this time, the missile was already travelling at over a thousand kilometres per hour, but in that super-stressed situation, it seemed to be crawling towards me in ultra slow motion. Strangely, I also knew that I had more than adequate time to avoid it.

When the missile was about 300 metres away, some heightened instinct urged me to bank the Alo. I just knew, at that precise moment, thanks forever to my overworked guardian angel, that the incoming projectile was locked on to the Alo's shiny left-hand main wheel shock strut extension, and that by pointing the shock strut directly at the supersonic missile, the shiny bit would be screened from the infrared sensor.

This action broke the lock-on, and although the missile continued towards us, it suddenly seemed to become confused and turn slightly to the left, which meant it passed just in front of the gunship, around six metres away. As it rushed past, I became entranced by its little guidance vanes shimmering in the supersonic airflow and its tiny movements as it sought vainly for a target to obliterate.

Then it disappeared. From the time the missile was fired to when it disappeared after passing my gunship, no more than six seconds had elapsed.

Back at treetop level, in the immediate aftermath of my close encounter with the SAM, the gunship formation regrouped and we took a decision by radio to resume the attack on the convoy, but with modified tactics. We agreed to form the normal wide attack circle around the target, but instead of going in at 600 to 800 feet (200 to 250 metres) above the ground, we would do so at treetop level. We knew this was outside the operating parameters of the SAM-7, and would make redundant any further use of missiles by the enemy.

The convoy was parked in the open at the eastern edge of the *shona*, which was surrounded by thick bush. Our plan involved each gunship, flying one behind the other and around ten seconds apart, to cut across the western side of the *shona* around 200 metres away from the convoy at low level. This would create a clear field of fire for around five to eight seconds, between exiting the thick bush on the northern side and regaining the cover of the bush on the southern side, for each of the 20 mm cannons firing from the left-hand sides of the Alos.

Done correctly, the bad guys in the missile-equipped GAZ trucks would be subjected to an extremely unpleasant and almost continuous stream of 20 mm cannon fire for around 60 seconds each time our formation passed by.

As tail-end-Charlie, this arrangement made it likely that I would experience the least hostile response from the convoy, provided that the damage caused by the first five gunships was effective. Conversely, if their damage was light, the enemy would be best prepared for my arrival when I wafted by at the rear of the formation.

As we were lining up a couple of kilometres north of the *shona* to start the attack, high above us, at an altitude of around 10 000 feet (3 000 metres), was an entity we all knew as Telstar. Flying in a light reconnaissance aircraft called a Bosbok, Telstar's role was to monitor activity on the battlefield. Whenever contact between SADF forces and anyone else was under way or imminent, Telstar would relay details of the developing situation to the brass in the SADF war room in Oshakati.

The gunships were already on the way in to the target when suddenly Telstar interrupted proceedings with an instruction that went something like this: 'Shotgun formation, this is Telstar. You are to immediately break off the attack on the convoy and return to the HAA.'

'What?!' said one of the Alo gunship pilots. 'These okes have been shooting the *kak* out of us and it's payback time!'

Someone else then said, 'There is a lot of interference and we can't hear you, Telstar.'

Telstar, urgency and tension apparent in his voice, shot back, 'Shotgun formation, I repeat, you are to break off the attack … I repeat … you are to break off the attack immediately!'

'No fucking way are we letting these fuckers get away!' someone said, echoing the thoughts of all 12 gunship crewmen.

'I know that you can hear me and this is an order. It comes from the highest authority in the land! Please stop the attack and go back to the HAA!' the concerned pilot in the Telstar pleaded.

A minute or so of stunned silence ensued as the leader of our formation led the gunships around the convoy in a wide circle but without firing at them. Then the lead chopper veered off to the west and the rest of us reluctantly followed.

The silence must have caused some degree of consternation all the way up the chain of command, as, every 20 seconds or so, the Telstar asked, 'Shotgun formation, have you complied? Please respond. Have you complied?'

It took a long time for the lead chopper to respond in the affirmative.

*

In the debacle that was Cuamato and its aftermath, I came to accept that the intensity of the Border War was escalating noticeably from operational tour to operational tour. From the middle of 1980 things escalated rapidly, and by mid-1981 the deployment of ever more sophisticated weaponry, particularly by FAPLA and PLAN, backed by the Eastern Bloc and Cuba, made the relatively safe operation and battlefield dominance of the Alo III gunship – which was, after all, only a converted Alpine rescue helicopter – a decidedly more perilous proposition.

From my point of view, 1981–1982 saw our aircraft being hit by enemy fire a lot more frequently than before, and there were fewer and fewer rest days back at Ondangs. There were more and more 'sleep outs' in places that were decidedly more hostile, with the number of joint operations increasing by the month, and with gunship crews having to work out ever more improved techniques and tactics to evade the sharp end of the enemy's opposition to our presence in southern Angola.

Until Cuamato, South Africa still adamantly maintained that our beef was with SWAPO and its military wing, PLAN, and *not* with the Angolan MPLA government or its armed forces, FAPLA. I don't know if I ever heard an official pronouncement of the rules of engagement for the SAAF when it came to FAPLA, but I, like all the other aircrews, was under the impression that if they shot at us, then we were entitled to shoot back.

Cuamato and its aftermath changed that. Despite the 1984 ceasefire agreed as part of the Lusaka Accords, the Border War soon resumed. The SADF continued to intervene in southern Angola, often in support of UNITA. Contact with PLAN was different, in that it had a stated objective to destabilise and attack targets in South West Africa, and South Africa had a duty to protect the citizens of that territory. Now that is about as deeply as I am prepared to go in discussing the legitimacy of South Africa's presence in the region.

At the time I firmly maintained, as I still do now, that the reason I became involved as a participant in the conflict was to forge an aviation career for myself. As my family lacked the means for me to fund this venture privately, the only really effective route open to me was through the military. I had always been resolute in the idea that, when I had accumulated the necessary hours, qualifications and experience to fly commercially, I would resign my commission and leave the SAAF.

By mid-1981, I realised that I still had quite a way to go to fulfil the minimum criteria for a career in the commercial flying industry. Though I had accumulated enough pilot-in-command helicopter hours, I was still well short of the mark where fixed-wing hours were concerned, and that was where, I believed, my future lay. Although I was reluctant to do so, I began to make discreet inquiries about moving away from the chopper environment and into the multi-engine transport fold as soon as the opportunity arose. It took almost another full year before I made the switch, and it took a change of command at 17 Squadron to help to accelerate my move.

My last year as an Alouette pilot was one of seemingly endless bush tours, a year in which too many friends and colleagues succumbed to the escalating hostilities, and a year in which I withdrew even further from the mould of the ideal military man.

Other factors also came to a head after Cuamato. The sentiments planted by Atie and others during the 1980 skiing holiday began to take root. As time went by, I found it more and more difficult to resist the instinct to question. After I got married I also felt it was unfair to subject my wife to the extraordinary stresses brought about by my frequent forays into the bush. I felt increasingly isolated, both at work and socially, without recourse to any form of support or understanding, even from professional counsellors. In fact, seeking counselling from anyone, amateur or professional, loved one or associate, was banned outright by the authorities and dire consequences were threatened for anyone found to have broken this rule.

I felt the need to watch my back more and more as my disdain for the apartheid government and its addicts became increasingly apparent and impossible to conceal. This is not a good thing when you are dependent on others, as occurs in combat.

*

Towards the end of 1981, I was sitting at a table in a crowded Durban restaurant having dinner with a very dear aunt when she asked me how I was coping with the death of my mom. I replied that I was still angry with my dad, whose behaviour in the years prior to Mom's stroke had, I felt, placed her under the extreme pressure that had led to the fatal crisis.

My aunt stared at me contemptuously for a few seconds, and then she leant across the table and slapped me hard across the face.

'You arrogant little bastard,' she hissed. 'Do you not know that your mother never slept a wink while you were in the bush? How do you think *that* affected her health?'

Up to that point, I'd never considered that I could have played any role in contributing to the rocketing blood pressure that had so cruelly taken my mom's life. My aunt's words and actions sent my mind into sudden shock. When I look back now, that incident in the restaurant opened the first tiny breach in my carefully constructed emotional defences and gave rise to a growing consciousness that ultimately put me on the path to leaving the SAAF.

But, mostly, I think I wanted out because at heart I sensed that I was and am a creator, a builder, perhaps even an idealist.

But I am not a soldier.

As I have got older, I have become a greater and greater pacifist and an avid supporter of conversation instead of confrontation. Yet, ironically, I am prepared to fight to the death, if necessary, to ensure that none of my children or grandchildren will ever have to experience the true horror of war.

Epilogue

I am now 60 years old. After leaving the SAAF in 1985, I abandoned aviation as a career and focused on building businesses instead.

The events described in this book happened almost four decades ago and, naturally, had a profound effect on my life. If I bear any grudge at all, it is against the military establishment, not for moulding me into the fighting man that I became for ten years by intentionally placing me in situations that required me to close down emotionally, in order to survive the experience, but rather because they blatantly shirked their responsibility to switch me back into a balanced, considerate and compassionate human being when my fighting days were over.

It would have taken little for them to have done so. Even if they had only acknowledged the possibility that so many of us young men (and a handful of women) had witnessed such untold horror that we required committed professional intervention to curtail further damage to ourselves and those close to us, in the ensuing years.

For example, my first marriage ended in an acrimonious divorce within five years of my leaving the SAAF. Also on the casualty list were most of the close relationships I'd forged over many years with friends and even family members, none of whom could understand or accept the random cold rage and overt callousness that seemed to underpin far too many of my actions, interactions and words.

Looking back now, I think I was hell-bent on trying to escape the claustrophobia of normal life with the legal means at my disposal. It is highly destructive to live your life in a state of permanent escapism, a state in which one establishes only tenuous bonds with those around you, never extending those bonds to an emotional level or even to partial intimacy. Keep things on the surface and it's unlikely that anyone will see the ugliness below, perhaps?

The worst of it all is that, at the time, I felt I was the only person around who was struggling to readjust, which just worsened the situation and made my withdrawal from those around me all the more complete. Knowing that something was very wrong and needed expert attention is one thing, but being legally barred from even approaching such experts was just plain cruelty. Even today, I know countless people who have really battled to adjust to life in South Africa after leaving the military, and many who are still in the fight. None of them sought the help they all so desperately needed but were barred from seeking.

Just recently, I had a meal with a close friend who was an ops medic from the same era. We have been friends for more than ten years and he has never once before talked about his experience. We were discussing my book when he suddenly began telling me of an incident involving a nine-year-old Ovambo girl who'd been caught in the crossfire during a contact between SADF and PLAN forces and had sustained multiple mortal wounds over her entire little body. She'd been airlifted by chopper, unconscious, from the battlefield to the surgical unit in which my friend and 15 other medical personnel were working. He recalled the terror in her eyes as she woke up in an alien environment, surrounded by masked medicos in blood-stained scrubs with shiny instruments in their hands, noisy machines in the background and the theatre lights glaring down on the operating table.

Forty years after the event my friend kept choking with emotion as he related the details of the tireless round-the-clock effort of those medicos as they frantically battled, with every bit of skill and each piece of modern science available, to save her.

But, despite their actions, on the morning of the fourth day she lost her final fight. These were men exposed daily to death and destruction and blood and guts and screaming and agony, but this particular incident profoundly affected them.

When she died, without being asked, each of the medicos from the unit chose to help to wash and clean the lifeless body of the girl. Then they dressed her in a pretty green frock that they bought from a local dressmaker.

My friend's final recollection is of the tiny bow tied at her midriff, fluttering in the wind, as her grandfather carried her off to bury her.

Until the day he told me this story, the trauma had remained hidden in a dark recess somewhere in my friend's mind. It seems to me that he, and so many like him, struggle to see that ridding themselves of the demons of the past is possible only by exposing those memories to the light.

My choice, made roughly five years after I left the SAAF, was to throw caution to the wind and see a skilled and experienced clinical psychologist. I never did confirm whether he diagnosed me with PTSD or not, but his intervention placed me firmly on a path to honestly confronting the dark stuff, and the resulting healing process re-awoke my inherent but dormant compassion and empathy.

Are all the ghosts of this period of my life buried? I'd like to think that they no longer dominate my life as they once did. It's become a lot easier to talk freely about most of those memories without my heart pounding too much and my chest tightening, but I also know that they will never fade completely.

A major contributing factor in my 'normalisation' is that, later, I also married my very best friend, Diane, and she has never shied away when I felt the need to talk.

This book is a continuation of that healing process. My story is but one of hundreds of thousands of stories in the minds of the southern African men of my generation, on all sides of the conflict.

I urge anyone who reads this book please to tell his or her own story, if only to someone who cares enough to listen.

It is never too late.

Acknowledgements

To attempt to name all of those who need to be acknowledged for their contributions to this book would be mightily unfair to those whose names I've neglected to include. I just trust that you know who you are and the roles that you played in moulding me.

Being surrounded by a loving family and good, solid friends while growing up is an extraordinary privilege, and the value of their support and guidance to me is simply inestimable.

The band of brothers (and occasional sisters) who had my back and afforded me protection and care during the operational years did so selflessly and without reward or personal regard.

I benefited enormously from those who taught me and I learnt so very, very much from those who fought at my side.

My thanks, too, to my publisher and the team at Delta Books, for making this book a reality.

Diane's patience with me while I wrote, and her often brutal honesty in critiquing my work, need a special mention and bottomless wells of my gratitude.

Mere words cannot adequately express my appreciation for the combined efforts.

Thank you one and all.